COSTUME
JEWELRY

Elvira López Del Prado Rivas

DT **DECORATIVE TECHNIQUES**

Schiffer Publishing Ltd®

4880 Lower Valley Road • Atglen, PA 19310

Original Spanish version published as:
Bisuterîa
Elvira López Del Prado Rivas
Parramón Publications Inc. 2007
ISBN: 978-84-342-2999-0
Translation by Omicron Language Solutions, LLC

Library of Congress Control Number: 2012951178

Designed by Mark David Bowyer
Type set in Frutiger / Souvenir Lt BT

ISBN: 978-0-7643-4149-6
Printed in China

Schiffer Books are available at special discounts for bulk purchases for sales promotions or premiums. Special editions, including personalized covers, corporate imprints, and excerpts can be created in large quantities for special needs. For more information contact the publisher.

Published by Schiffer Publishing, Ltd.
4880 Lower Valley Road
Atglen, PA 19310
Phone: (610) 593-1777; Fax: (610) 593-2002
E-mail: Info@schifferbooks.com

For the largest selection of fine reference books on this and related subjects, please visit our website at:
www.schifferbooks.com
You may also write for a free catalog.

This book may be purchased from the publisher.
Please try your bookstore first.

We are always looking for people to write books on new and related subjects.
If you have an idea for a book, please contact us at:
proposals@schifferbooks.com

In Europe, Schiffer books are distributed by:
Bushwood Books
6 Marksbury Ave.
Kew Gardens
Surrey TW9 4JF England
Phone: 44 (0) 20 8392 8585; Fax: 44 (0) 20 8392 9876
E-mail: info@bushwoodbooks.co.uk
Website: www.bushwoodbooks.co.uk

COSTUME
JEWELRY

Contents

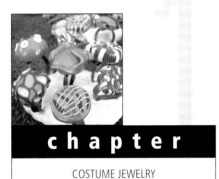

4

chapter

COSTUME JEWELRY
MADE WITH FELT TECHNIQUES

5

chapter

COSTUME JEWELRY MADE
OF POLYMER CLAY TECHNIQUES

6

chapter

COSTUME JEWELRY MADE
WITH PAPER AND CLOTH

Introduction

hen tackling a book about costume jewelry, with step-by-step details, the first task is to set some parameters around the subject and concentrate on one area. Due to the incredibly broad sphere of this field, impossible to condense into just one book, we have focused all the projects on making costume jewelry inspired by hand craft and made up of unique and independent pieces. These pieces will undoubtedly be central to your future jewelry creations, inspired by the following exercises. The first chapter leads the way towards opening up the mind and artistic eye to the new forms of creative expressions that will be discovered throughout this book. Starting from the notion that our most basic working equipment is in fact our own hands, the second chapter will look in depth at the different materials and tools we have at our disposal to aid us in our work. There are also explanations of the different uses for each tool, according to the task at hand and the desired result. Next, each chapter concentrates on making pieces of costume jewelry in a different material: wire, felt, polymer clay, paper, and cloth. These pages show, in clear detail, various techniques for working with each of these materials, accompanied by a short section that shows the possible variations on the techniques previously explained. Lastly, there is a gallery of images displaying work by international artists, all of which is made with the materials discussed in this book.

—Elvira López Del Prado Rivas
Jewelry and Costume Jewelry Designer

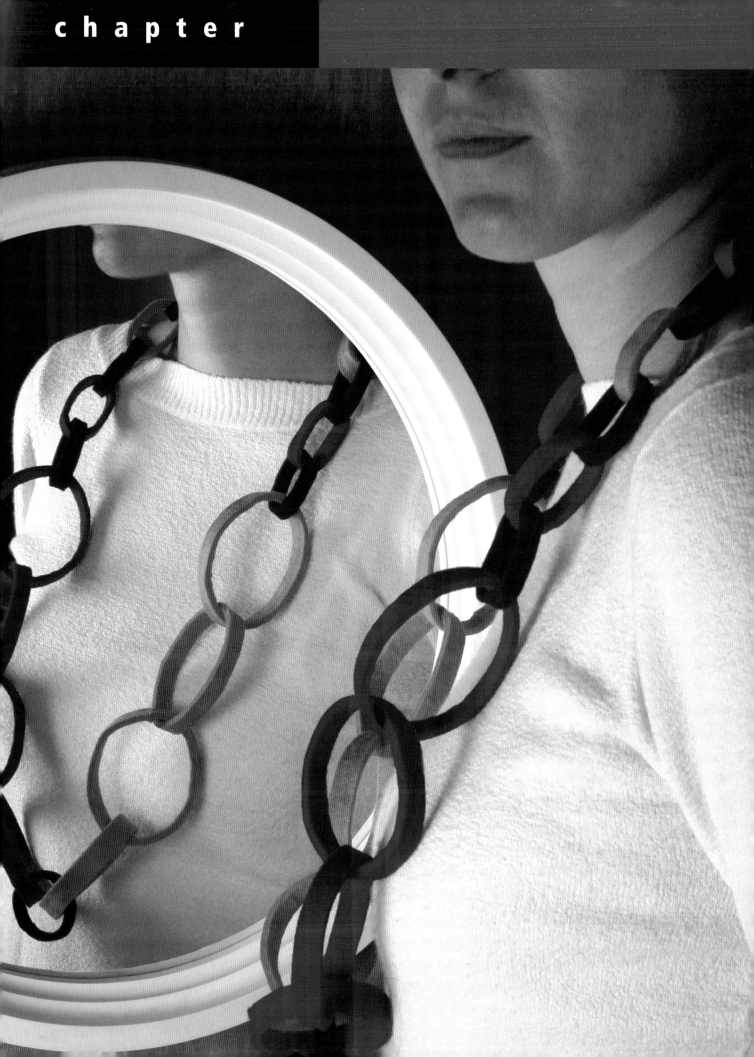

Costume Jewelry

Over the years costume jewelry has undergone conceptual
changes that reflect society's intellectual development.
Initially conceived of as an imitation of traditional jewelry
in non-precious materials, the concept was then developed
further. Sometimes it has faded into the background due to
lack of dialogue with developments in fashion, and at other
times, as has happened in the last few decades, it has played
a remarkably important role in the world of accessories. Part
of the intellectual and psychological development of human
beings is based on the recognition of one's own identity. This
identity, which we present to the rest of society, is formed to
a large extent by our clothes and accessories, which mark
us out and integrate us into a social group. The traditional
hierarchical gap between jewelry and costume jewelry has
almost disappeared due to the creation of different types
of jewelry.

History

The history of humankind cannot be told without mentioning costume jewelry and fine jewelry, which share the same origin. From prehistoric times, human beings have felt the need to adorn their bodies. At times these objects were symbols of warfare or protection, but in most cases they have used personal adornment as emblems of power and authority. As people evolved as individuals, and their needs developed, so too has the history of costume jewelry. This section will go back to the beginnings of the concept of costume jewelry and look at how it has evolved.

Beginnings

In Prehistory, objects for personal adornment were very basic, as human beings used all the things that were easy to find and manipulate, such as stones, mollusk shells, conch shells, bones, fossils, seeds, etc. The oldest beads, which have lasted until today, were found by Professor Christopher Henshilwood of the University of Bergen in Norway, and date back some 75,000 years. They are known as Nassarius beads, and were found in Blombos Cave, South Africa. They are part of a necklace of mollusk shells, each pierced in the middle, and they still have the mark from the thread that they hung from. As human beings have evolved, we have learned to distinguish, gather, and work other more precious materials such as coral or metals; on the other hand, the development of tools and their specialized use has made the creation of ever more beautiful pieces possible.

Reproduction of the *Nassarius beads* found in Blombos cave, South Africa.

Necklace of seeds from South America and necklace of glass beads from South Africa.

Costume Jewelry

Before the 1920s, jewelry was something designed for the aristocracy, the nobility, and royalty, who wanted to show off pieces made with valuable materials and precious stones.

Each public act or social gathering was a showcase where the ladies of high society had the opportunity to show off adornments of luxurious gowns and valuable jewelry.

There was jewelry designed and made for each occasion, and not only necklaces, brooches, rings, or bracelets, but also dressing table items such as boxes, combs, brushes, and even hairclips and hatpins. With the rise of the middle classes, situated half-way between poverty and wealth, which established a new and growing clientele, the demand also came about for low and mid-price products. Therefore, between 1920 and 1930 the production of mass-produced costume jewelry with ordinary materials, different from those traditionally used for jewelry, was developed. This opened up the existing gap, still apparent today, between extremely conservative traditional jewelry, which uses metals and precious stones, and costume jewelry, which is daring and innovative, both in terms of techniques and materials.

Piece of costume jewelry from the collection of Barbara Berger. When fashion designers included costume jewelry in their collections it was taken really seriously.

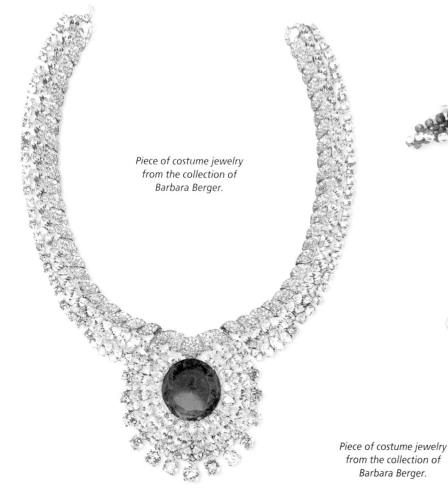

Piece of costume jewelry from the collection of Barbara Berger.

Piece of costume jewelry from the collection of Barbara Berger.

Fashion and Trends

Contemporary costume jewelry is viewed as a clothing accessory and is sold by fashion labels designed for a young teenage public. Displayed as essential items in the shop windows of high street stores, these pieces of costume jewelry have accessible prices and a short shelf-life, and just like fashion, tastes and trends that vary from year to year.

Alongside this mass-produced high street costume jewelry, there is also costume jewelry made by up-and-coming designers. It is much less mainstream and more cutting edge, and is made with people who are open to challenging conceptual boundaries in mind. For this expressive costume jewelry-jewelry hybrid, all materials are suitable—recycled or not, attractive or not, paper, plastic, glue, etc. It goes

as far as the creation of pieces that are impossible to wear to the office or when taking the children to school, due to the materials used, or the size, or just because they are conceptual works bordering on the sculptural and conceived of as being exhibited in a gallery and not worn.

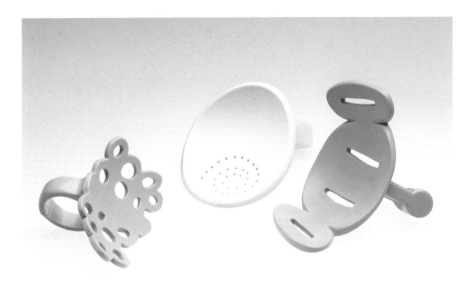

Cloud, colander, radiator, part of "The cup as ring" series, plastic, **Sarah Kate Burgess, U.S.** All the work from this artist is full of meaning; it is never a work put together by accident. This work comes from the belief that everyday objects are designed as ornaments for the human body.

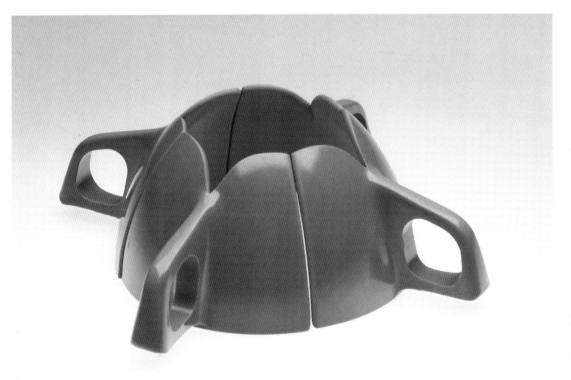

Set, also belonging to "The cup as ring" series, plastic, **work by Sarah Kate Burgess, U.S.** This artist calls for a reconnection to the charm of everyday life.

Moss bracelet, plastic, **work by Ineke Otte, Holland**. Artist and designer, not only of jewelry. This artist is inspired almost completely by nature, from where she takes colors, shapes, and textures to achieve her sinuous and evocative pieces.

Garden ring, Plexiglas, acetate and silver, **work by Burcu Büyükünal, Turkey**. Colorful and amusing pieces filled with colored drinking straws.

Bubble ring, ABS plastic (polyurethane mold), **work by Arthur Hash**.

Plexiglas, acetate and silver bracelet, *work by Burcu Büyükünal, Turkey.*

Hot Glue Necklace, strands of hot silicone glue, *made by Arthur Hash*.

Orange Bag Bracelet, plastic, **work by Arthur Hash, U.S.**

Resin necklace. **Made by Elvira López Del Prado, 2007, Barcelona, Spain.**

Brooch made in polymer clay and brass. **Made by Elvira López Del Prado, 2007, Barcelona, Spain.**

Inspirations

There are many ways of developing artistic creativity. Influences from different stimuli can provide you with inspiration to work from. Each creative process is attached to a stimulus that has been a trigger to set inspiration in motion. The search for these stimuli has been a fixation throughout history and all human beings have the capacity to react to beautiful things. Any situation can automatically trigger inspiration.

The Design

An idea is born from inspiration and this idea is what must be recorded as soon as possible in a notebook. It is a good idea to always carry a sketchpad or notebook with blank pages available to put down all the ideas and inspirations that cross your path. Even, if possible, stick in pieces of the things that inspire you: a flower, some photos, a postcard, some words... It is also a good idea to do a small sketch of the piece in mind. Even though it is time-consuming, you will have the idea set out in your notebook before commencing a project. Along with creating a design on paper, you can also make an initial model in a modeling material such as Plasticine®.

Section of the painting, *La Primavera*, by Sandro Botticelli (circa 478). The three graces have been represented innumerable times by artists in all periods. They symbolize the goddesses of charm, grace, and beauty, constant sources of inspiration.

Models for projects, sketches, and notes that
will be useful for developing a project.

Various books on the history of jewelry from its
origins and books, with step-by-step explanations
that can be very useful as sources of inspiration.

Still life made of souvenirs,
postcards, and objects.

Do-it-yourself

In the last few years, an artistic and non-artistic trend has grown inspired by the alternative DIY movement. This new marketing concept has advantages for the consumer and for the company selling it. On the one hand, someone buying a product with the label "do-it-yourself" knows that he or she has the advantage of it being cheaper, and companies use this concept as an incentive for sales marketing to make assembly costs cheaper. This trend has spread to costume jewelry. Based on this concept, shops have sprung up all over the world specializing in advice about and sale of articles and tools designed for the client who wishes to make his or her own creations. As well as actual stores, there are also Internet pages on the web where anyone can access tutorials that can be downloaded free. These tutorials give step-by-step explanations for making costume jewelry with the most diverse materials and techniques. It is possible to find blogs on the web that allow for active participation and the exchange of knowledge and ideas between users.

Ring Stitch, from the collection "Do It Your Self," paper, **work by Sarah Kate Burgess, U.S.** According to their creator, the appeal of these pieces of paper jewelry is found in the experience of making each one by hand.

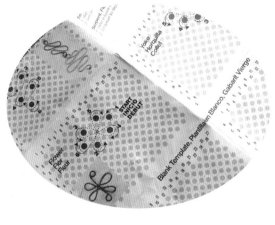

Guide from a Jig maker that explains how to do filigree work.

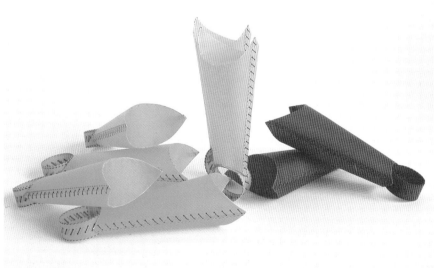

Ring Patch, from the collection "Do It Your Self," paper, **work by Sarah Kate Burgess, U.S.** The pattern for these rings can be downloaded free from her website.

Costume jewelry beads made with resin by the students on a do-it-yourself costume jewelry making course.

A display of rings in polymer clay, made by following the instructions on various Internet blogs.

Different tutorials from Internet blogs giving detailed step-by-step instructions to using various polymer clay techniques.

Some students working on creations of their own designs.

Found Objects

This field of costume jewelry follows the same principles as those of the fashion industry, meaning that it moves at a dizzying pace. Fashion is a fleeting industry, with trends blossoming and dying many times in the same year. The colors, the material, and inspirations are in constant flux. Costume jewelry goes through these same changes. One of the longest lasting changes throughout the last few trends is the art of making pieces from found objects. Such objects are hardly changed; they are adapted, respecting their original use as much as possible. And that is where their appeal lies, in being pieces "stolen" from other uses in order to form part of costume jewelry accessories. These "finds" are viewed by educated eyes as recycled art.

Tussie Mussies, 2000, **work by Natalie Lleonart.** Brooches made from pieces of old costume jewelry.

Twinset Necklace, 2003, **work by Natalie Lleonart.** Necklace made with old colored knitting needles.

The book of risks: taken and untaken, 2002, copyright, 18 carat gold, copper and multiple processes, **work by Alyssa Dee Krauss.**

Necklace with two 1950s porcelain balls.
These pieces were found in an antiques market.
Elvira López Del Prado.

Various found objects ready to be transformed
into pieces of costume jewelry.

Snapped belonging to the "Accumulation" series, **by Sarah Kate Burgess**. These
pieces combine golden decorative elements taken from old postcards with drawings
of hazy shapes and luxurious necklaces. They are given meaning and importance
thanks to the fact that they follow a design plan, according to the artist.

Twinset bracelet, 2003, **created by Natalie Lleonart.** Made with old colored knitting needles.

Crack belonging to the "Momentary" series, **work by Sarah Kate Burgess, U.S.** Conceptual work with which Sarah Kate Burgess tries to provide a wider view of personal adornment. Belonging to a series of works where daily objects are structured into enormous ornaments.

Bracelet made only with palm leaves, **work by Elvira López Del Prado, Barcelona (Spain), 2007.**

Primavera Necklace, made from decorative garlands. *This work is by Elvira López Del Prado, Barcelona (Spain), 2007.*

Festive necklace. This was created from recycled Christmas decorations. *It is a creation by Elvira López Del Prado, Barcelona (Spain), 2004.*

Resin rings and beads made from old photographs and found objects, *creation of Elvira López Del Prado, Barcelona (Spain), 2005.*

Ring made with a river stone decorated with window color and a button.

Tools
and Materials

There are many tools in varying forms on the market for making costume jewelry. For this reason, only the specific tools required for each job at hand are shown here. The aim of the current chapter is for you to familiarize yourself with these tools and the basic instructions for using them. Again, the tools described here are specifically those needed for the step-by-step explanations. Please note, there are nearly infinite varieties of these tools, each adapted to a particular need on particular pieces.

This chapter also provides advice on how to plan and organize a small workshop, and the best way to light it.

The Costume Jewelry Workshop

When talking about a workshop for costume jewelry, people probably imagine a large space full of boxes and tools. However, in actual fact, to start off you can use your house, adapting the dining room or kitchen table, as long as there is good lighting. One of the advantages of making costume jewelry is that the materials and tools used are small and require little workspace and storage.

Organization

A good work table and a chair with a comfortable back are very important, otherwise you will damage your back by prolonged poor posture. You must both rest your back on the chair from time to time and not stare at small pieces for long periods. To make the work easier, it is a good idea to have all the equipment, jars full of findings, tools, etc., on hand.

Having various small boxes with separate compartments to keep all your materials, tools and findings organized is very practical, as it allows you to arrange your workspace and move the materials easily. A good organizational trick is to order these objects by family, color, and size, so that you can find what you need quickly, so you can have your own workspace.

Transparent jars and pots for organizing and locating findings.

Different boxes with separate compartments are very practical for carrying around small materials.

Organization
of tools.

Lighting

Lighting is very important and has to be taken into account by anyone working for long periods of time with very small pieces that need to be looked at close up. The ideal lighting is natural light. Position your chair so that the light comes from behind and from the left if you are right handed or the right if you left handed, so that your hands do not cast shadows. If there is no natural light, the best solution is to combine indirect halogen light with an adjustable table lamp that directly throws light on your hands.

Light from behind and the left side is the best lighting for working if you are right handed.

Tools

There are various tools used for costume jewelry; here, they are divided into basic and supplementary tools. In these sections, you will find other tools subdivided according to their function. You will see how some household items can help with making costume jewelry. All these tools are easy to find in hardware stores and specialist stores. Household items can also be found in the supermarket.

Basic Tools

Basic tools refers to those tools deemed essential in a costume jewelry workshop when working with the materials described in this book.

To make them easier to recognize and store, they are ordered according to their practical function: cutting, fixing, supports, adjusting, and supplementary.

Cutting Tools

As the name suggests, these are tools designed for cutting different materials. There are specific cutting tools for each material, such as scissors, knives, cutters, and pliers, which will be explained in the following section. All these materials are found in hardware stores and handicraft stores.

• Scissors
These items can be found easily. They do not need to have any special characteristics, but they must be well sharpened.

• Cutters
Used for dividing up polymer clay, cutters should preferably have a wide handle, which allows you to press down and achieve a clean cut. They should also be well sharpened.

• Cutting pliers
Especially useful for cutting metal that is not very thick. This book will show you how to use them to split copper wire. These are also sold in hardware stores, in various sizes and shapes, according to the thickness of the wire needing cutting.

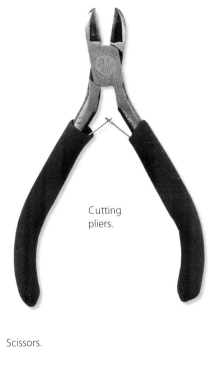

Cutting pliers.

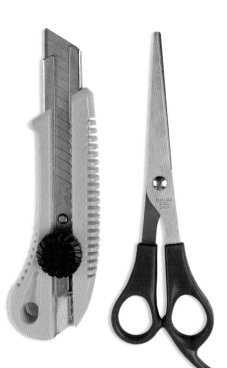

Cutter.

Scissors.

• Metal cutters

These are useful for making clean cuts on polymer clay without pushing it out of shape. They come in a wide range of shapes and sizes. You can find them in stores specializing in products for working with polymer clay. They are made in metal or plastic, with metal ones being the most suitable as their edges are sharper.

Cutters of different sizes and shapes.

Fixing Tools

This category includes tools used for piercing or for work with cuts or holes: felting needles, thin sewing needles, wool needles, and engraving punches.

• Wool felting tool

This tool consists of a handle, which can be made of wood, plastic, or metal, into which various needles for felting are introduced. Each of these needles has small protrusions at the end that facilitate the felting process. The tool with four needles is used for working on larger felt surfaces and the tools with one needle are used for filigree work or surfaces needing more accuracy. The appearance of this tool varies according to the manufacturer. Working with needles requires extreme care, as they are very sharp.

• Thin sewing needles

These are the needles traditionally used for sewing clothes. In the exercises in this book, sewing needles will be used often, at times to join pieces of felt when it is impossible to stick them together with glue, and also to sew together remnants of cloth.

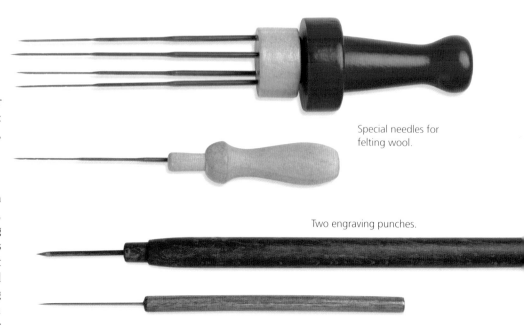

Special needles for felting wool.

Two engraving punches.

• Wool needles

These needles are the same as the previous ones but a little bigger, as they are used to sew garments made of wool. As they have a very large eye, they are very practical for pushing cords through balls of felt with the help of pliers.

• Engraving punches

A punch is made of a piece of wood, normally with a sharp metal end used in engraving to make indentations in the metal. Punches are useful for making holes in pieces of polymer clay. They can also be used for decoration, making textures and indentations.

Various thin needles and wool needles.

Supports

Listed here are the basic support tools used to hold pieces of costume jewelry while you are working, such as jigs, bolts for coiling wire, ring measurers, anvils, and synthetic foam.

• Jig

The jig is made of a board covered with holes with pegs of varying thickness in some of the holes. It is usually square, round, or rectangular, and generally made of plastic or metal. This tool is used for working with wire of different thicknesses, and allows for a number of pieces to be produced.

• Wire coiling bolt

This tool is used to coil wire. It is often called a "Coiling Gizmo" or "Twister," after two of the many products on the market. Basically, they are used to make spirals of different sizes. For this reason, the tool has different interchangeable pieces. You can find detailed instructions for its use where you buy it. In the section dedicated to wire there is an exercise using a coiling bolt. The result is very professional.

• Ring measurers

These are long sticks in a slight pyramid shape on which there are, usually, marks for the different ring sizes as well as their size in millimeters. They come in metal, plastic or wood. Those made of plastic and wood have the advantage of weighing less. Being lighter, ring measurers are easier to carry, and those made of metal are more suitable for working with wire as they hold the pieces better.

Plastic Jig.

Metal Jig.

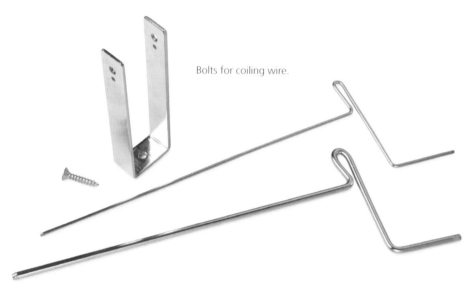

Bolts for coiling wire.

• Small anvil

The anvil is a piece of solid metal used for supporting small metal pieces, which will be hit with a mallet, also of metal, with the aim of flattening the wire. It is a good idea to use it on a surface fixed to the ground or even on the ground. You can put a towel over it to muffle the blow and not make too much noise.

• Synthetic foam

This is used for felting wool with needles. This process is done by hammering the needle in the wool a number of times, so a soft base is needed to stop the needle from breaking. The foam should be at least 2 3/4" or 3" (7 or 8 cm) thick.

Synthetic foam.

Ring measurers.

Small anvil.

Mallet and hammer.

Adjusting Tools

These are all the tools that change the physical or chemical characteristics of the material. In fact, almost all tools change materials in some way, but those explained next are designed specifically for this purpose: mallets, hammers, sandpaper, pasta making machines, domestic ovens, and heat guns.

• Mallets and hammers

There is a wide range to choose from depending on the material to be hammered. Those mallets and hammers used in the step-by-step instructions are for hammering and flattening wire. You should always change the size of the mallet to match the wire or the piece being made.

• Wet sandpaper

These sandpapers come in a wide range of weights. The size of the grain is specified on the back of each piece of paper with a number. The smaller the number, the larger the size of the grain on the sandpaper. When sanding, always start with a small number (depending on the damage or state of the piece) and finish with the highest, 1000 or 1200, for example. They are called wet sandpaper because they are used under the water or damp so that they are not too abrasive on the material. In this book they are used for working with polymer clay, so sandpapers of numbers 320, 600, and 1200 are used.

Pasta making machine.

Heat gun.

Wet sandpaper.

Electric oven.

• Pasta making machine

This machine is actually used in the kitchen to make fresh pasta, but artists using polymer clay have found it is ideally suited to help in making perfect sheets, which are the base of many techniques for working with polymer clay. This device is made of two rollers that can be opened up to varying degrees; this opening is different depending on the make of the machine.

• Electric oven

When working with polymer clay it is essential to have an electric oven to fire the pieces. It must have a thermostat and a timer.

• Heat gun

This tool is used for working with polymer clay. Applying heat to a fired piece increases its shine. Therefore, if you work with translucent polymer clay or liquid clay, once the piece has been fired in the oven you can use it to apply heat with the gun to increase its transparency and shine. It is possible to use it as the only form of firing, but it is preferable to fire with an electric oven, so that the pieces become more resistant.

Supplementary Tools

Supplementary tools are all the items, conventional or not, that can at one time or another help in your work. The next section focuses on those tools useful for undertaking the exercises in this book: pliers, jewelry tweezers, a pencil, and an eraser.

• Pliers

All of these are useful for holding, although the shape determines their use. Chain nose pliers are used for holding the wire and gripping the crimp beads and clasps of necklaces. Pliers with a flat nose are for holding large pieces and crimping, those with a long chain nose are for holding and crimping, and those with a round nose are for doing twisting work with wire; these last pliers are very useful for opening and closing jump rings without breaking them.

• Jewelry tweezers

Used for working with beads and for holding the material you are working with. The most basic pair opens when squeezed. When these tweezers are not squeezed, they hold the pieces in place.

• Pencil and eraser

It is a good idea to have these at hand, as they are used to make marks on felt and on paper.

Various jewelry tweezers.

Chain nose pliers (A), flat nose pliers (B), long chain nose pliers (C), round nosed pliers (D).

Pencil and eraser.

Extra Equipment

On these pages you will see other tools usually used for other household tasks, such as clothes pins, plastic jars, place mats, etc., but which can also be useful for costume jewelry work. Here they are divided into support tools and supplementary tools.

Supports

In this case, basic support tools are not professional tools but are everyday objects, such as aluminum foil, clothes pins, wooden sticks, methacrylate, and some pots.

• Aluminum foil

Aluminum foil is an ideal material for covering the oven tray, as it stops the flat pieces being fired from getting dirty. They are also used to give internal structure to balls of polymer clay. First you make the aluminum ball and then cover it in polymer clay, making the balls weigh very little and also not using a lot of material.

• Towels

Towels are used to work with wet felt, stopping the water from spilling all over the work table. It does not need to be a particular kind of towel, but you should bear in mind that some felt dyes run and could stain the towel.

• Clothes pins

These are very useful for firing balls in the oven. Preferably made of wood, they are placed one in front of the other to hold a metal rod full of balls of polymer clay.

• Skewers

These are used to hold pieces whilst they are being varnished or when doing *découpage* work. They should be round, and made of wood or metal. They are inserted into the hole of the piece to hold them more easily.

• Methacrylate board

This allows you to shape the polymer clay without leaving unsightly indentations, letting you see how the piece is coming along. It should not be very big, as it needs to be easy to hold when pressing down on the clay to flatten it. Any hard, smooth surface will suffice, such as the cover of a CD, a small mirror, etc., but not wood, as it will leave imprints of its texture in the clay.

• Circular jar

These are used to work with wire. These are used as a base when working with wire. In exercises that involve wire work, however, you can use any geometrical base that you wish, without it necessarily being round or plastic. You can use any material and any hard base.

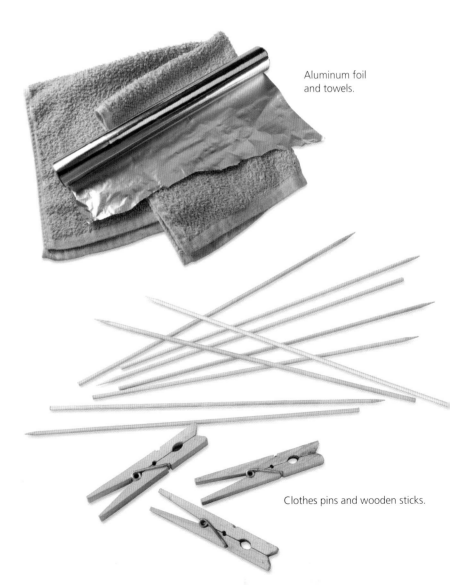

Aluminum foil and towels.

Clothes pins and wooden sticks.

Methacrylate board and round plastic jar.

Supplementary Equipment

When you are making costume jewelry, you will probably need tools or equipment belonging to other artistic disciplines, such as metal rods, modeling sticks, paintbrushes, bowls, and bamboo place mats.

Bamboo place mat and bowl for water.

• Thin wire rods

They are used for holding the balls of polymer clay in the oven whilst they are being fired. The thickness of the rods depends on the size of the hole in the balls. Use, for example, pieces of copper wire, and lay them across some clothes pins.

• Modeling sticks

These sticks are designed for modeling and adding texture. They are made in plastic or wood; both materials are suitable if they are very shiny and smooth. The sticks are usually used for working with cold porcelain (also called Russian porcelain) to give texture. They are used for modeling and giving textures to clay as well and they are found in handicraft shops.

• Paintbrushes

Paintbrushes are useful for applying patinas, varnishes, and glue, as well as working with découpage. They must have fine soft bristles.

• Bamboo place mat and a bowl for water

The bowl and the bamboo are used for working with wet wool felting. The method for this will be explained later on.

Thin wire rods.

Sticks for modeling and giving texture to wood and plastic.

Fine soft haired paintbrushes.

Materials

The following pages explain in detail each one of the materials needed for making the costume jewelry shown in this book. These materials and the tools for working with them are divided up according to their use so they are easier to identify and recognize. The materials section has been divided into three broad groups: main materials, extra materials and findings, and threads and beads.

Main Materials

Felt, wire, polymer clay, paper, and cloth make up the group of main materials and the extra materials will be explained afterwards. There are some very diverse materials among them, some of which are not traditionally used in costume jewelry. There will be a brief overview of the history of some of these materials in order to better understand their usual uses.

Earring made of a knitted tube of copper and clay polymer. *Work by Elvira López Del Prado.*

Design and creation of brooch made of a knitted copper tube and polymer clay. *Elvira López Del Prado.*

Reels of enameled copper for wholesalers, 1,000 m.

Wire

Metal is one of the oldest materials known to have been used in jewelry making. Copper, gold, and silver were some of the first to be found and, therefore, also the first to be worked with.

In the form of wire, which is made of thin threads obtained by stretching the metal, there are pieces of jewelry in existence dating back to 2000 B.C., made entirely in copper wire. Such pieces belong to the ancient Sumerians. Likewise, pieces made of copper wire have been found in some ancient Egyptian tombs, which are estimated to be around 4000 years old. The Romans also knew different techniques for working with jewelry made of metal wire. Even the Vikings discovered how to make metal chains without soldering.

Even after the invention of soldering, jewelry made with metal wire was still used as it was cheap to make. Afterwards other metals appeared that were the result of copper alloys—for example, bronze = copper + tin, brass = copper + zinc (among others). Another metal often used for costume jewelry is pewter, which is a result of an alloy of copper + tin + antimony. It is a shiny metal with a color similar to silver. Also,

nickel silver, which is a result of an alloy of copper + zinc + nickel + tin. All these metal wires are very popular in costume jewelry. Nowadays, there are others that do not cause allergic reactions: for example, niobium, titanium, surgical steel, or anodized aluminum; the latter being made enameled in colors and sold under the name Magic Wire.

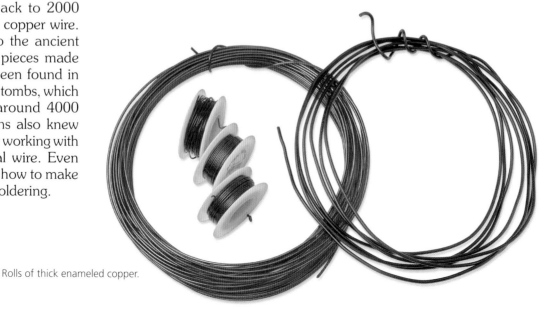

Rolls of thick enameled copper.

• Enameled copper wire

Enameled copper wire is sold on reels, which have between 72 and 3280 or 4000 feet (22 and 1000 or 1200 meters), depending on the manufacturer. You can buy it as required. It comes in a wide range of colors and in different sizes. To start, it is a good idea to choose some reels of only a few feet in order to have a wide choice of colors and gauges, as the reels with more feet are more expensive. Starting from .040" (1 mm) thick, copper wire is very hard to work with, but it gives very durable and long lasting results. There are other types of copper wire which are very attractive. For example, copper covered in colored plastic or tubes of knitted copper.

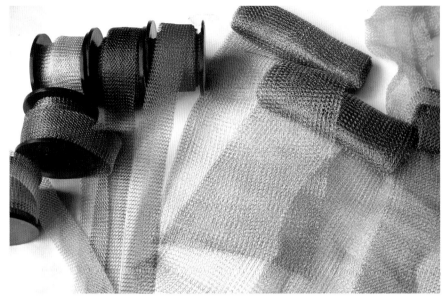

Rolls of wire of various sizes.

Reels of wholesale, 18 to 24 m., enameled copper.

Copper covered in colored plastic.

• Anodized aluminum wire

This wire comes in different colors and sizes. It is much softer to manipulate than copper, making it easy to model using greater thicknesses. It is sold in specialty stores in coiled feet and reels.

• 925 silver thread

The thickness will depend on the pieces you are going to make. The most flexible threads range between .028" and .040" (0.7 and 1 mm). Less than .028" (0.7 mm) is a little fragile and more than .040" (1 mm) is too hard. It is possible to find silver with an alloy of 930; in this case, you can choose a size of .020" (0.5 mm), as this silver is stiffer. The threads are usually sold in feet, but this depends on the store.

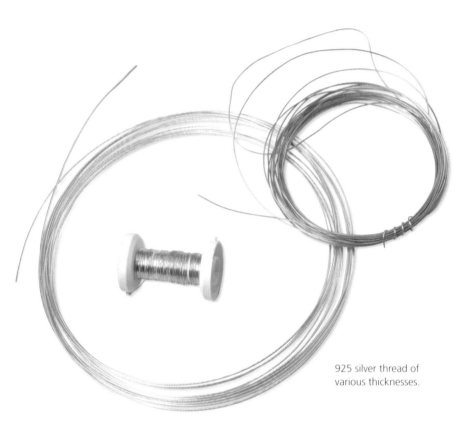

925 silver thread of various thicknesses.

Anodized aluminum wire in different colors and sizes.

Felt

The origins of felt are uncertain, but there is archeological evidence going back to millions of years B.C. It was probably discovered by accident, but it was most certainly nomadic tribes in Asia who first used it. Sheep were shorn to make felt with their wool, and this material helped the nomads to endure difficult weather conditions.

Each fiber of the wool is formed of tiny flakes that open up when rubbed. If this rubbing is accompanied by hot water and neutral soap the process greatly speeds up. When the flakes open up, do not allow the fibers to disentangle, and when they cool and dry they will stay stuck together, making felt. The internal cells of the wool repel the water whilst those outside absorb the damp. This property makes wool a very warm material.

Skeins of unfelted dyed wool.

Sheets of industrial felt
1 cm thick.

Herd of Merino sheep.

Detail of the difference in thicknesses
of manufactured felt.

Sheets of manufactured
felt, 3/32" (0.5 cm) thick.

To manufacture felt, a basic method has been developed based on thousands of needles perforating the wool at the same time to make felt without the need to use soap and water. Needles can also be used for felting wool manually or for making decorations. In the chapter on felting techniques, you will find this process explained step-by-step. Two thicknesses of felt are worked with in this book, .196" (0.5 cm), called thin felt, and the other, which is thicker, .393" (1 cm), called thick felt. For costume jewelry work, it is recommended to use good quality felt, which can be found in stores specializing in this material.

Bracelet and bag made by weaving strips of packaging.

Paper and Cloth

The use of paper and cloth is not very popular in costume jewelry and jewelry; however, there are artists around the world who base creations on these materials.

Pieces made in paper and cloth are often manufactured and handcrafted, as, due to their physical characteristics, they need to be adapted somewhat in order to be worked with, for example, by gluing or varnishing both materials. When using paper, it is a good idea to use a very thin variety, such as that of a paper handkerchief, whilst with cloth, any type can be used.

This chapter is dedicated to these materials, centering on three basic techniques: découpage, paper recycling, and a type of patchwork called "fuxico," whose use is quite widespread in Brazil. This technique is also known as "jo-jo" patchwork; it is used for making bedspreads, pillows, and clothes, and some artists use it to make costume jewelry.

Some indigenous people in Mexico have developed an eye-catching technique that involves weaving strips of sweet wrappers to make accessories and costume jewelry..

Necklace and brooches set made with fuxico patchwork technique. *Work by Joan Scott, U.S.*

Glass tray with cake case serviettes on a background textured with metallic paint. *Piece made by Rosa and Mercé Oller* using *découpage*. Barcelona, 2007.

Polymer Clay

Polymer clay is a thermoplastic polymer called polyvinyl chloride (PVC), made from two natural raw materials: 57% sodium chloride or common salt (ClNa) and 43% hydrocarbons. Therefore, this clay consists of a type of plastic material that polymerizes (the particles fuse together) with an increase in temperature, and stabilizes when it reaches 266°F (130°C), although this depends on the manufacturer.

This material appeared in Germany during the 1930s thanks to Fifi Rehbinder, who developed the formula in order to make her dolls, and sold it under the name of Fifi Mosaik.

The Eberhard Faber Company bought the formula in 1964 and sold it under the name Fimo® (from FIfi MOsaik). Fimo was sold in Europe in doll stores and in the 1950s it was exported to the U.S. From then on, polymer clay gained in popularity and spread to other expressive and creative fields, including jewelry.

At the beginning, polymer clay could only be made in white, and handicraft makers had to color it with pigments. Nowadays, this is not necessary as there is an extensive range of colors and shades.

It is also possible to mix different makes without any problems. Polymer clay can also be colored and painted before and after firing, and once fired and cool, it can be sanded, drilled, and fired again if necessary.

In general, the colors of polymer clay do not alter with firing, but there is a line of translucent colors that do change when fired in an oven. This range comes in various shades and, as its name suggests, becomes translucent once fired.

If heat is applied directly with a heat gun, you can make them totally transparent and greatly increase their shine.

The different manufacturers and handicraft makers have been improving and modifying the formula to develop

Box with dividers, which is very practical for keeping polymer clay pieces in.

more specialized finishes; depending on the use and requirements of the pieces, you can choose different formulas.

For making sculptures, there are special mold making clays that are very flexible. There are even clays for making erasers. They are found in very large formats.

• Polymer clay in liquid format

The liquid format is sold in plastic containers on which each manufacturer indicates the firing temperature. It has a milky, doughy appearance. This type has various functions: such as a softener for polymer clay, as glue between two pieces of clay, as varnish, it can even be dyed.

There is also a multitude of decorative techniques for polymer clay with a liquid format base.

Polymer clay in liquid format.

• Polymer clay with mica powder

Clays that contain mica can be recognized because they shine slightly in the light, as this powder gives a metallic appearance and texture to the polymers.

Mica is a mineral found naturally in the earth. It is not toxic and has a neutral pH, but it should not be inhaled, as it contains other metals such as aluminum that could be dangerous.

Mica powder draws dampness out of the clay, drying it out, therefore you need to work it a little before using it, either with a rolling pin or pasta machine

• Storing polymer clay and keeping it clean

This material will usually last quite a while open, but you should take the precaution of keeping it in hermetically sealed boxes in a dry place out of direct light.

In the summer it is advisable to store it in a plastic box with a lid, such as a lunch box, and keep it in the fridge, so that when you cut it, the cut will be clean and it will not go out of shape.

In winter, on the other hand, the clay becomes very hard and difficult to work; in this case, you can apply the heat gun to it for a few seconds or leave it on the radiator for a few minutes to give it consistency.

In terms of cleaning, you must always keep the work area clean as polymer clay is a material that easily picks up particles of dust and dirt. To stop some colors staining others, you should also clean your hands and the table with wet wipes or paper dampened with alcohol.

Special clays with glitter.

Clay in translucent colors.

Polymer clay in neutral colors.

Polymer clay with mica powder.

Additional Materials

This section is divided into "supplementary materials" and "surface materials." The latter are varnish, polish, asphalt, transfer paper, soap, glue, and super glue.
Supplementary materials are only used for particular techniques and surface materials include all those that will alter the surface or exterior appearance of the pieces.

For Surfaces

These materials are the ones that are applied last, when the piece is completely finished. When they are applied to costume jewelry they alter its surface or exterior appearance. Amongst them are patinas, varnishes, gums, glues, etc.

• Varnish
The varnish used depends on the desired finish and the material being used. It is sold in tins of approximately 8 1/2 fl oz. (250 ml) tins for handicrafts. There are synthetic or acrylic, shiny, gloss, or matte varieties, and depending on the manufacturer the finish of the pieces will vary significantly. They are sold in drug, handicraft, and specialty stores.
The varnish used in making the pieces in this book is synthetic, transparent, and shiny, and gives the pieces a very eye-catching finish.

• Asphalt (a.k.a. Bitumen of Judea)
Asphalt is used to age or darken pieces, in the exercises in this book it is used with polymer clay. It is sold in specialist and handicraft stores.

• Liquid polish
Used with polymer clay once it is fired and sanded. It is sold in 8 fl oz. (200 ml) tins, especially for handicrafts. It is applied with a natural fiber cloth, massaged into the piece, and then the excess is removed with a clean, dry cloth. The objects acquire a beautiful shine and become silky to the touch.

• Paper to transfer images to cloth
This paper reacts to heat. It is often put on with an iron, but in this book it is put directly into the oven, as it is used with polymer clay. The temperature for this clay is shown on each block, but is around 266°F (130°C) for about fifteen minutes. Print the image that you want to use onto the paper, following the manufacturer's instructions. It is sold in packets of ten sheets in usual printing paper size.

• Neutral soap
This is used especially for wet felting, as it facilitates and speeds up the process. Bar and liquid forms can be used.

• White wood glue
The appearance varies depending on the manufacturer, but it is usually sold in plastic containers and looks white and creamy. Glue diluted in water is used for paper découpage in the chapter dedicated to that material. A container of 8 fl oz. (200 ml) is sufficient.

• Super glue
Super glue should be used with caution. In the book it is used for joining sheets of felt. It can give off irritating vapors when it comes in contact with the felt, due to the colorants used to dye the wool, so it is advisable to use tweezers to pick it up. Super glue comes in various sizes from 3 to 8 grams and is sold in different containers: tubes, with a brush applicator, etc. All can be used.

Supplementary Materials

Included in supplementary materials are sewing threads and fine nylon thread. It is a good idea to have a wide range of colors and a variety of shades of sewing thread, if you are going to do costume jewelry in cloth. When using nylon, it is advisable to use one of 0.15 mm to sew flat felt if super glue is not suitable.

Varnish, polish, and asphalt (above).

White wood glue and super glue.

Bars of neutral soap.

Transfer paper.

Findings,
Threads and Beads

Last but not least, there are all the pieces designed to finish off pieces of costume jewelry. This section includes all types of beads and baubles, threads, wires, cords, and more, as well as all the findings that will be needed, at one time or another, to finish off your work. The section will show some of the more common examples, but there are many more on the market.

Findings

In the following section there will be a brief overview of the most common findings. All of them are easy to find and depending on the specialization of the store are simple or elaborate.

• **Earring bases**
There are two different types: flat bases, which are stuck onto a bead or piece made in felt, polymer clay, etc. and cross bases, which are made of four rods soldered to the main part of the earring for setting a bead in, as one of these rods has a small hook for this purpose.

• **Earring backs**
They are to stop the earring falling out. There are metal versions and also silicon ones to avoid allergic reactions. They fix on to the back part of the earring, so that they are hidden behind the ear.

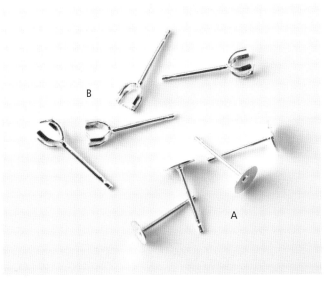

Earring bases, flat (A) and cross (B).

Earring backs.

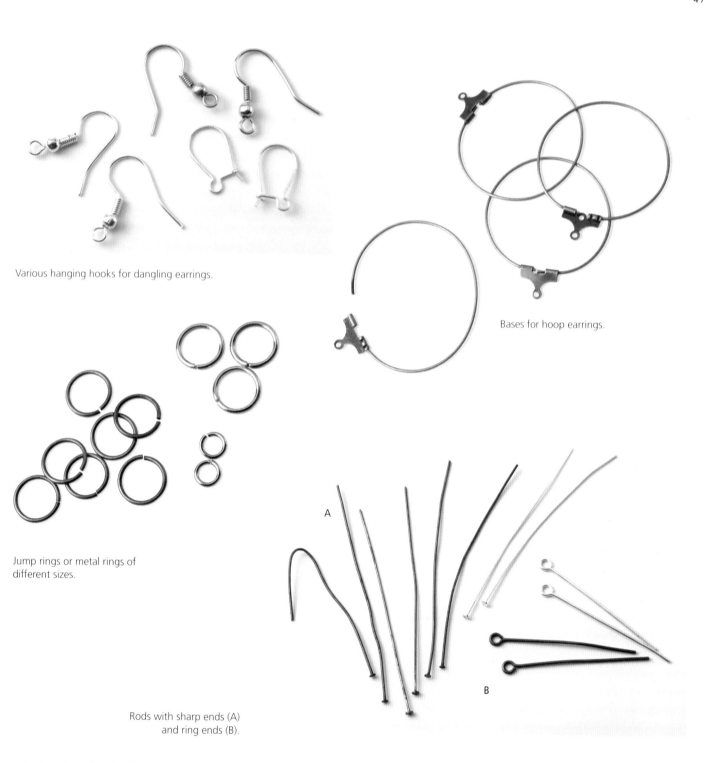

Various hanging hooks for dangling earrings.

Bases for hoop earrings.

Jump rings or metal rings of different sizes.

Rods with sharp ends (A) and ring ends (B).

• **Various hanging hooks**
These hooks are used especially when making earrings with pieces that dangle from the ear. They often have the basic shape of a hook or harpoon, depending on the manufacturer.

• **Rod**
This is used to hold beads in place. Basically, it is made of a metal stick joined to a flat piece, like a pin, or soldered to a jump ring. These are the basic types, but you can find other designs depending on where you buy them.

• **Jump rings or metal rings**
A circular metal piece with an opening that can be manipulated. It comes in different sizes and can be used to make chains, to join pieces, or even to fix the ends of necklaces.

Crimp beads of different sizes.

End cover or shell

Different clasps: ball and ring toggle clasp (A), lobster clasp (B), spring ring clasp (C), and hook and eye clasp (D).

Other necklace clasps (A) and (B) and caps (C). These are used for thick cords or large pieces.

Spacing bars.

• Crimp beads
Small metal balls with a hole, which are flattened with flat nose pliers. They have various uses; for example, they are flattened to close necklaces made with threads or cords and also for clasps and decoration.

• End cover or shell
Metal piece with a hole at the side whose function is to improve the appearance and cover the ends made with crimp beads. Depending on the manufacturer, there is a wide variety available.

• Clasps
Clasps are metal pieces put on to the ends of necklaces, pendants, or bracelets. There are various types of clasps, including lobster, spring ring, hooks and eye and ball, and ring toggle. All of them are used to finish off necklaces and bracelets and should be chosen for their thickness, the material of the threads, and cords used. The manufacturers bring out new models each season, which can be found in stores.

• Spacing bars
Metal pieces with holes used for creating spaces on a necklace or bracelet threads. They are also very decorative when used independently to assemble earrings with rods and beads; they are quite simple to manufacture.

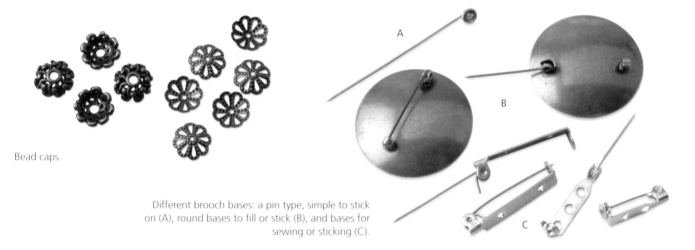

Bead caps.

Different brooch bases: a pin type, simple to stick on (A), round bases to fill or stick (B), and bases for sewing or sticking (C).

• Bead caps
Metal plates in the shape of a cap. There are many different types and they are used for covering up the ends of beads; if they are round then they fit better.

• Bases for brooches
There are different bases for brooches: needle types that are simple to stick on, round bases for filling or sticking, and bases for sewing or sticking. There are many types depending on the supplier.

• Ring bases
A wide range of bases for rings are available. They are often made of a cylindrical base, with a size that can be changed, stuck to a flat or semi-flat base, onto which you can add a piece of costume jewelry.

• Other bases
Bases of other materials, such as methacrylate, plastic, wood, metal, etc., can be covered with polymer clay and fired together in the oven or they can be covered by découpage.

Different bases for adjustable rings.

Base for a methacrylate bracelet.

Metal bases for filling with polymer clay.

Threads

It is important to spend some time getting to know and explore the range of threads and cords on the market. They are made in a wide variety of designs, colors, and materials, as well as formats, depending on the manufacturer. Likewise, and following fashion trends, each season new models go on sale.

The design of your piece, the size of the hole in the beads, the time of year or the color are factors to consider when choosing an appropriate thread, but in fact the only pattern to follow is your own taste.

Threads come in various thicknesses and should be matched up with the size of the hole in the beads being used; likewise, think about the weight of the pieces and choose a durable thread that goes with your costume jewelry. The next section describes some of the most common types.

• Nylon threads
These are sold in various thicknesses and colors as well as the transparent variety. Nylon is used for bead rings with a pattern (Swarovski-type) and for necklaces of beads close together where the thread is not seen or for bracelets with a clasp. They are very strong.

• Elastic cord
Elastic cord can be found in a variety of colors and also a transparent version. There are different thicknesses to choose from depending on the size of the hole in the beads. It is better to use them in bracelets without a clasp, but not in necklaces, as they often cannot take the weight of the beads.

• Tiger tail cable
This is steel covered with nylon. It comes in a wide range of colors and in various thicknesses, and it often worked with crimp beads. It should not be bent as it easily gets out of shape. It is used when the thread forms an important part of the design of the necklace, as it is very elegant.

Nylon thread and invisible elastic thread.

It is sold in multiple foot reels or by the foot.

• Memory wire
This is a metal thread, of a spring type that is cut to the size you need, as it adapts to the size of the neck, finger, or wrist. It is called memory wire simply because it goes back to its original shape. Necklaces, bracelets, and rings are made with it, and it is ideally suited for being covered in beads.

• Stiff choker
Circular piece of metal with an integrated clasp, usually used to make necklaces formed out of a single piece. They are sold individually or in sets of various pieces.

Tiger tail cable.

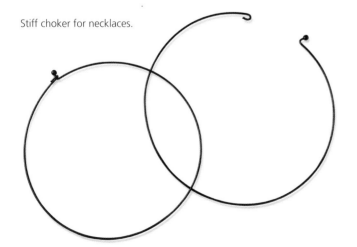

Stiff choker for necklaces.

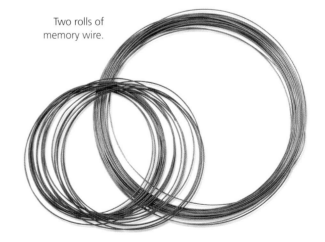

Two rolls of memory wire.

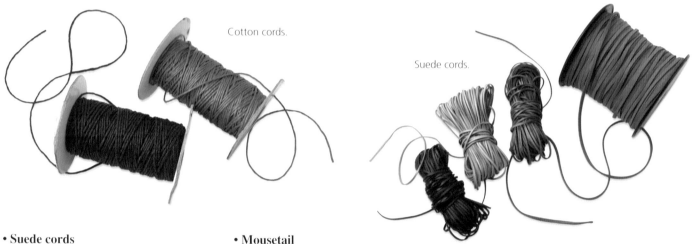

Cotton cords.

Suede cords.

• Suede cords
This is usually flat with a soft matte finish. It comes in a variety of widths and colors. It is often used when working with a lobster claw clasp.

• Cotton cord
These are made of various layers of threads, which can be lightly waxed. They are well suited for use in the spring and summer.

• Leather cord
These cords come in a variety of thicknesses and colors, synthetic or natural, and also waxed. Use them according to your taste and the balance of the piece.

• Mousetail
A very silky and shiny cord, ideal for making costume jewelry with Chinese knots.

• Linen thread
These threads are sold waxed and unwaxed. They are often used for making summer costume jewelry.

• Organdy ribbon
It comes in various thicknesses and colors, with a feel similar to gauze. It is very elegant and is even used in combination with pearls.

Leather cords.

Various rolls of mouse tail cord.

Linen threads in different colors.

Colored organdy ribbon.

Beads

Beads are all the perforated pieces that make up part of a piece of jewelry or costume jewelry. Each bead, depending on its origin and material it is made from, has its own name: glass beads, seed beads, bone beads, wooden beads, etc. There are also beads made from resin, a synthetic material with a warm feel used to imitate other materials. Beads come in a multitude of shapes and sizes; they offer as many possibilities as your imagination allows.

Coral resin beads (A), turquoise Arizona beads (B), bone beads (C), tropical seeds (D).

Tiny glass or rocaille beads.

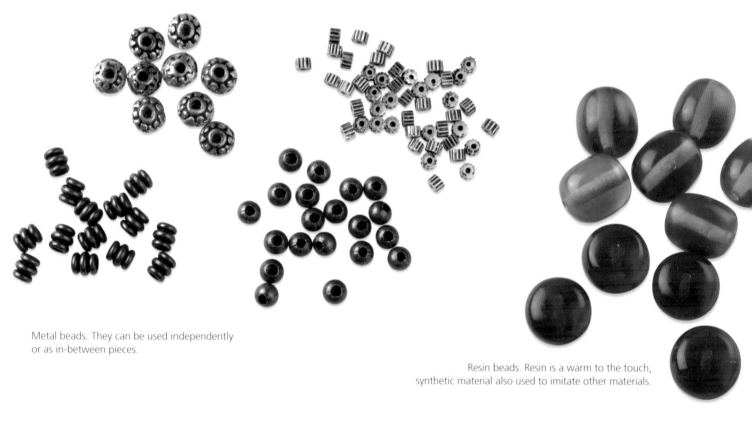

Metal beads. They can be used independently or as in-between pieces.

Resin beads. Resin is a warm to the touch, synthetic material also used to imitate other materials.

Different colored glass beads.

Costume Jewelry
Made with Fire

This chapter shows different
projects that can be tackled when
using a malleable and compliant material like
enameled copper wire. Usually used in the electrical and
telephone industries, today it is found on the jewelry market
in a wide range of colors and thicknesses suitable for
adults and children. Thanks to its flexibility, very
eye-catching results can be achieved in a short
time. The costume jewelry projects in this
chapter use wire and some other
decorations.

Techniques

Working with copper wire is not very complicated, if you keep some basics in mind. The ends constitute an important part of the finish, as they have to be well hidden or camouflaged for the piece to be considered properly finished. On the other hand, ends made with wire are very useful for decorating a piece of jewelry. The right tools for the thickness and size of the wire being worked on must be used. Do not use pliers that are serrated.

The Ends

This term is often used in costume jewelry when referring to the two end parts of the same piece of cut wire. When finishing a piece made with wire, you need to hide the ends if you can, which means putting them through the hole of the nearest bead or between the threads of the same piece.

Sanding and gluing

When it is not possible to hide the ends, they need to be "camouflaged" as much as possible. The final professional appearance of the piece depends on this. In specialty jewelry supplies stores and sometimes in well stocked hardware stores, special sandpaper for metal can be found, which is used for sanding the tips of the ends still visible.

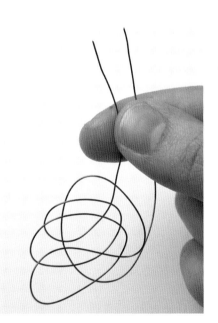

The ends.

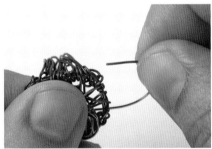

Ends hidden inside the ring.

Sand the tip until it is rounded so that it does not prick.

A drop of super glue can be applied to fix the end of the piece.

Hardening

When you want a particular piece to be harder than it is, you can choose to hammer it with a suitable mallet or hammer on a small anvil. If you use a very thick copper wire, 1 to 3 mm, you should make it into the desired shape before hammering it. Then hammer it, making the blows progressively stronger until the desired result is achieved.

Piece of 1 mm silver. If the metal is heated beforehand, it is easier to model it with a mallet.

When the piece uses a very thin wire you must choose the right hammer and use a smaller one so it does not break.

Wire Finishes

Wire is not only used as a basic material for making pieces of costume jewelry, but also as decoration, to imitate filigree on large beads.

The next section will show how to make glass beads more eye-catching with the help of copper wire.

Various examples of decoration with wire.

1- Use a small bead to fix the wire at the base of the large bead.

2- With some round nose pliers twist an end over itself to make a rounded shape, creating a hook.

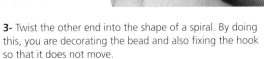

3- Twist the other end into the shape of a spiral. By doing this, you are decorating the bead and also fixing the hook so that it does not move.

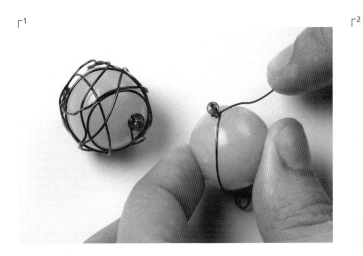

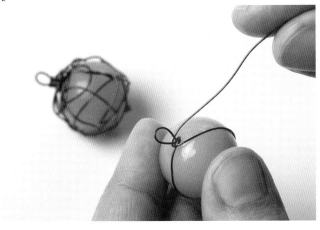

1- As in the previous example, fix the wire to the large bead with a small bead.

2- Make a hook. Twist the end around itself a number of times.

⌐3

⌐4

3- Pass the wire through the hole of the large bead a number of times, and from there begin to interweave it around itself.

4- Hide the end with the help of pliers.

⌐1

1- Make a hook using some round nose pliers. Twist it around a few times.

⌐3

⌐2

2- Insert a small bead and thread an end of the wire through each end of the large bead you want to adapt.

3- Tighten it well and cut the leftover ends.

The thread has been passed through the hole of the bead a number of times to create this elegant basket.

Projects

This section shows how to make six pieces of costume jewelry with enameled copper wire in different sizes and colors. The following steps will show you various ways of working with the wire, from which you will be able to make as many adaptations as you can think of.

Although the following projects are made primarily with wire, large beads and small beads have been added to make them more attractive and fun.

Grappolo Ring

The Italian word *grappolo* means "bunch," as at first glance these rings look like bunches of fruit.

The basic technique is very simple, involving incorporating beads and placing them around the ring. Although traditionally these beads are round and of the same color, this next exercise is a variation on this. Beads of different sizes, colors, and shapes have been mixed together to create a very dynamic piece of jewelry that is easy to wear with casual clothes.

To make the grappolo ring you need a ring measurer, wire and beads. The wire is a chocolate brown color, 0,6 mm in diameter, and the beads are of different materials: turquoise, glass, wood and seeds, and go very well with the color of the wire.

⌐¹

1. Cut approximately 3 ft. (1 m) of wire and put it around the measurer, leaving one end shorter than the other. Work with a length three sizes bigger than the ring you want to make. Due to the characteristics of this ring, when it is finished it will have decreased three sizes.

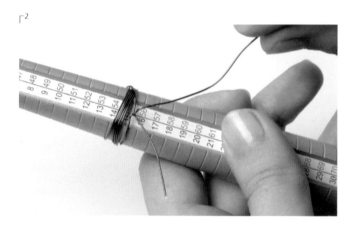

2. With your thumb, hold the short end while winding the wire around the measurer a number of times with the other hand. Connect both wires together by twisting them.

3. Thread on some of the beads you have chosen.

4. Keep dropping beads onto the wire and winding it around the measurer, arranging the beads in a harmonious fashion.

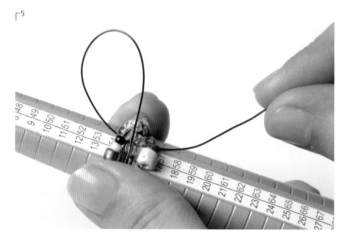

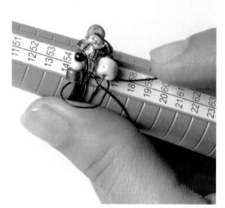

5 and 6. After putting the first beads on, affix the wire of the ring so that the beads stay fixed without moving. You can repeat this a couple of times, as it also has the function of decorating the ring.

7 and 8. Put more beads on, alternating shapes and colors on the wire. Put them on at the same time as winding the wire around the measurer. You can include a piece with a large hole and, for decorative purposes, thread the wire through it several times.

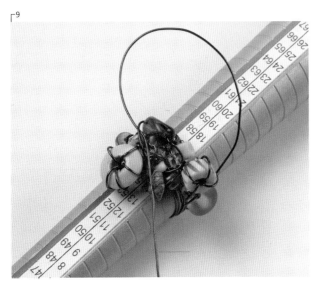

9. Once you have decided that you do not want to add any more beads to the ring, secure the wire a number of times to make sure that it is properly set, and that it will not move around when you remove it from the measurer.

10. As a last decorative option, you can use the round nose pliers to make some interesting twists on the copper on top of the beads.

11. Lastly, take the ring of the measurer and set both ends by twisting in a spiral. Camouflage the ends.

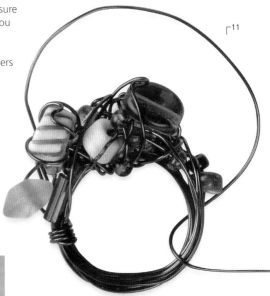

12. The ring is very eye-catching due to its color and shape. An interesting detail is the piece in the shape of a wheel added to the design, as the position can be changed easily with your fingers.

Crisscross Necklace

These pieces are rather stylish. To make them you need geometric shapes for support. Cylinders, squares, and rectangles are ideal and very easy to find amongst household items. The basic technique of this necklace is one of the most creative, as it allows you to create many different varieties with few resources.

First choose the color. In this case, the chosen wire for the outside is black and 0.025" (0.6 mm) in diameter, and purple wire, 0.0159" (0.4 mm) in diameter for the inside, small glass beads in mauve and red, and a cotton cord, also red.

1. Use a round box as a base, and wind the black wire, which has been cut to 4' (1.20 m) long, around it several times, leaving one short end and one long end. Depending on the thickness of the thread, wind it around a little more or a little less, with the aim of making the piece durable.

2. Twist the threads together to fix it to the base.

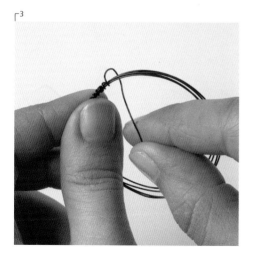

3. Take the piece off, cut the short end, and begin to wind the long end around the base that you have made.

4. Once you have gone around the whole circle, cut the end with pliers.

⌐5

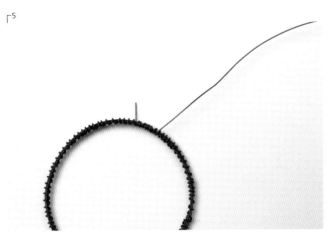

5. Next, cut 3' (1 m) of the purple thread and wind it around the circle you have made a few times to secure it.

⌐6

6. Pass the purple wire around the base evenly, turning the wheel around as you do so.

7. Secure the thread to the base at times to stop the wires from moving about.

⌐7

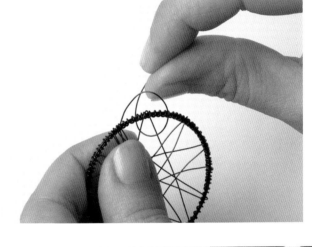

8⌐

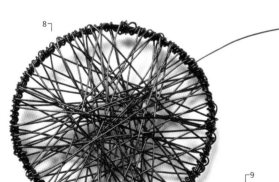

⌐9

8. Spread the wire out well until you have a design similar to the one in the photograph. Leave a loose piece at the end of about 10″ (25 cm) long. Depending on the distribution of the thread, the resulting design will vary considerably.

9. Insert all the beads onto the end.

10. Let them drop and distribute them at the same time as you wind the wire around the base, until there are no more beads left. All the beads must be on the same side of the necklace.

11 and 12. With flat nose pliers secure the final end a number of times to the outside of the necklace.

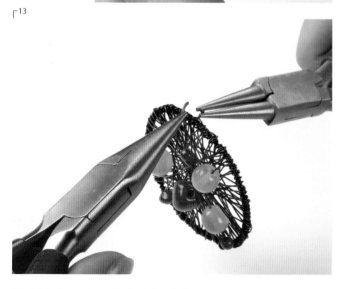

13. Add a jump ring with the help of pliers.

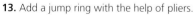

14. Cut various pieces of the red cord to size and thread them through the jump ring.

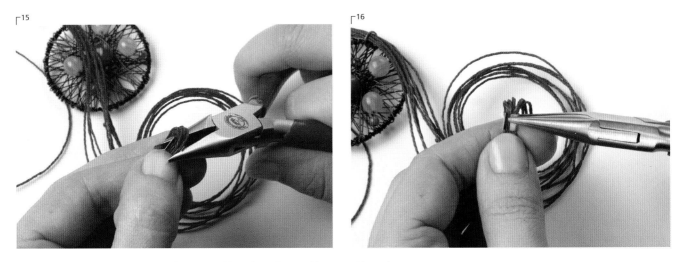

15 and 16. With the help of pliers, fix on a necklace clasp designed for use with cords.

17. Lastly, fix a jump ring at each end of the clasp, together with the lobster claw.

18. The result is this simple necklace suitable for people of all ages.

Spiral Earrings

In this project you are going to work step-by-step to create spirals of different thicknesses by hand. You will create jewelry that is perfect to wear on any special occasion. Jewelers use drills and specialized electrical tools for this type of work. Here, you will obtain similar results, but by using more accessible tools for someone wanting to start out in the techniques of costume jewelry.

Enameled copper wire in a chocolate color, 0.0126" (0.3 mm) in diameter, silver thread 0.025" (0.6 mm) thick, hooks for earrings, and metal beads. You will use the wire coiler for making the spirals.

1. Without cutting the end of the roll of wire, secure it with a couple of twists to the thinnest rod.

2. Pass it through the corresponding hole and begin to wind it.

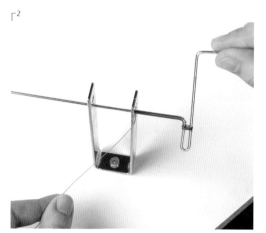

3. Once the rod is all wound with the wire, take it out.

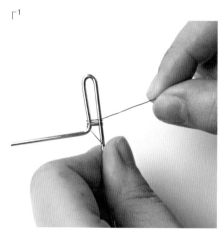

4. Cut a piece of the silver wire, about 12" (30 cm), approximately. Introduce it into the spiral until it reaches the center.

5. Adjust the spiral to the size of the silver wire. To do this, make the spiral twist from one end to the other

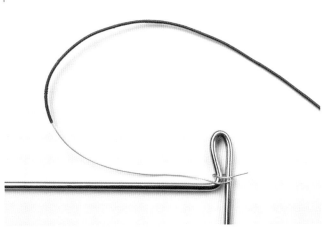

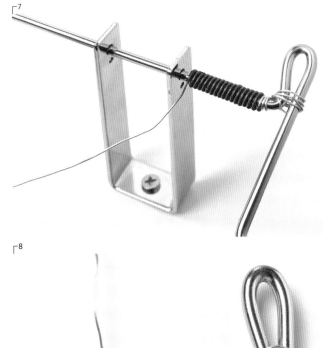

6. Take the thickest rod of the coiler and secure the silver wire with a couple of twists, in the same way as before.

7. Introduce the rod into the corresponding hole and wind it until it cannot wind any more.

8. To finish off, wind the silver wire the same number of times as you did at the beginning.

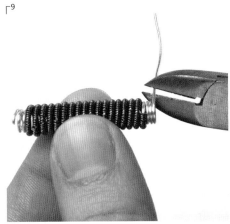

9. Take the piece out and cut the leftover ends.

10 and 11. Cut 3" or 3 1/4" (7 or 8 cm) of silver wire, push them through the earring to check the length, and make a jump ring with pliers.

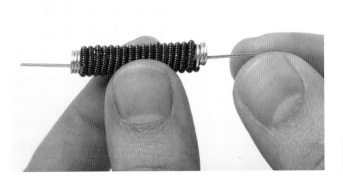

12 and 13. Push this piece through the earring again, and at the other end repeat the operation, including a metal piece as decoration.

14. Lastly, put an earring hook on, also silver so as not to clash.

15. This is the result once both earrings have been made following the same process step-by-step.

Jig Bracelet

Simplicity and elegance define this bracelet, which seems to have come from an Ancient Greek archeological site. This piece shows that with just a few materials it is possible to emulate the most classical of tastes. An ideal bracelet for everyday use that, with a contemporary appearance, is very tasteful.

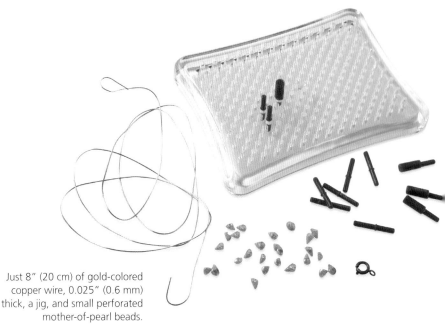

Just 8" (20 cm) of gold-colored copper wire, 0.025" (0.6 mm) thick, a jig, and small perforated mother-of-pearl beads.

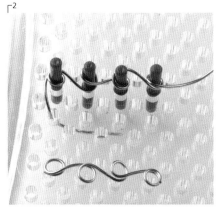

1. Put four thin rods in a line, without spaces, and wind the thread in the direction shown in the picture.

2. Cut the leftover ends. Make two equal pieces.

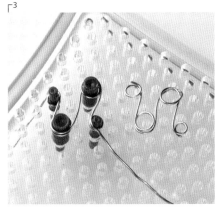

3. In the same way, and following the diagram in the picture, make three pieces like this.

4. Harden them by hammering them with a mallet, taking care not to break them.

5. With round nose pliers, make a figure eight with the wire. Insert on one of them two of the 1/2" (1 cm) mother-of-pearl beads. For the bracelet, you will need six pieces like this, but you do not need to harden the others.

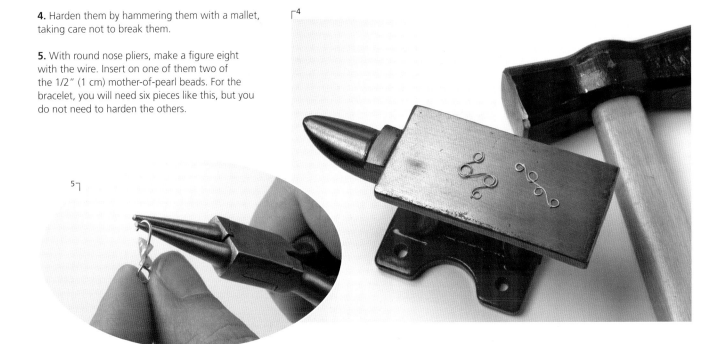

6. Organize all the pieces to check the order they will be in when putting the bracelet together.

⌐6

L7

7. Begin to hook some of the pieces with others using pliers.

⌐8

8. The result is a simple and delicate piece of costume jewelry.

Baroque Ring

This section will demonstrate another way to use a jig. The instructions are very detailed, as the shapes used here are more complex than those of the previous project. You can alter the size of the ring by varying the placement of the pegs in the jig. Use the ring measurer as the base.

You will need a jig, enameled copper wire, 0.025" (0.6 mm) in diameter, and Bohemian glass beads.

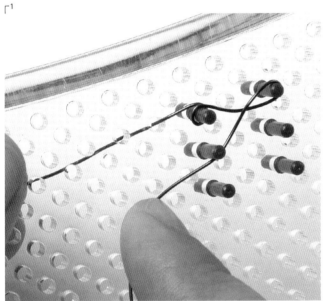

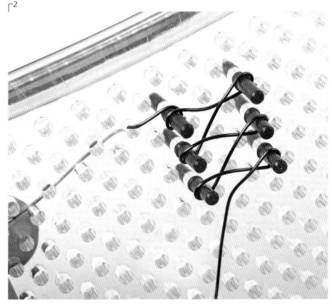

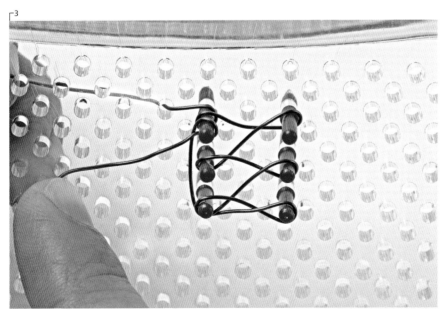

1. Make a square with six narrow pegs placed in two parallel lines, and wind the wire by making circular shapes between them.

2. The result should be similar to this.

3. Take the copper wire upwards to form a side wall and wind it around the far right peg.

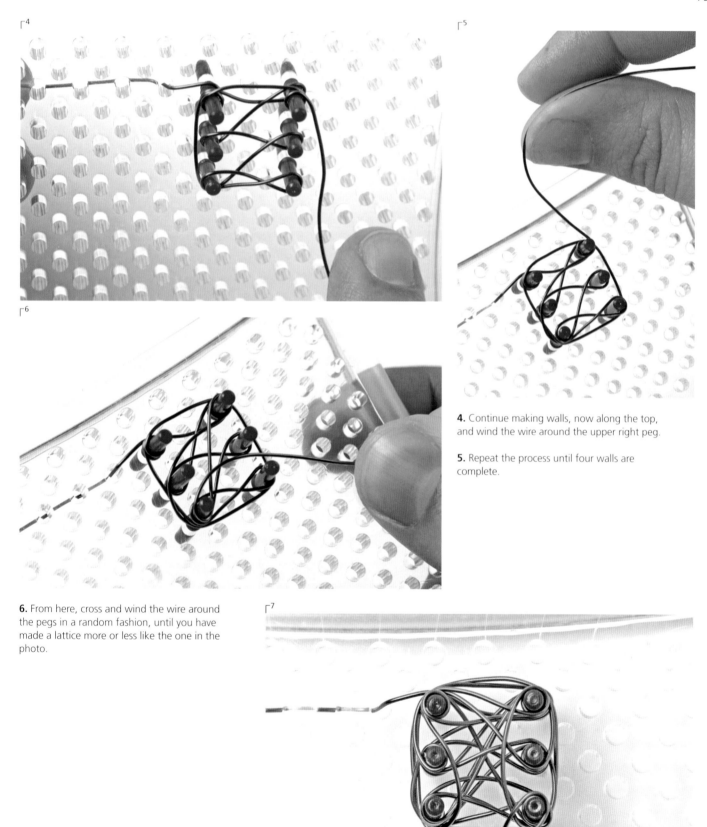

4. Continue making walls, now along the top, and wind the wire around the upper right peg.

5. Repeat the process until four walls are complete.

6. From here, cross and wind the wire around the pegs in a random fashion, until you have made a lattice more or less like the one in the photo.

7. According to where you have wound the wire, the design of the lattice will change.

⌐8

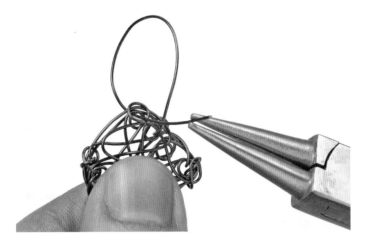

8. Take the piece off the jig and secure the whole piece by putting the wire around it; thereby making sure that the design does not go out of shape.

9⌐

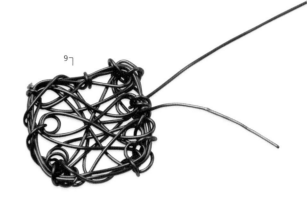

9. Cut another piece of emerald green wire about 28" (70 cm) long and fix it to the base.

⌐10

⌐11

10 and 11. Put the piece on the ring measurer, this time on the correct size, and begin to pass the wire underneath the measurer and from one end of the ring to the other, always securing it underneath as shown in the picture.

⌐12

12. Once you have finished winding, put on one of the Bohemian glass beads.

13. Fix it to the base by twisting the wire around it.

14. Take the ring off the measurer and camouflage the end by hiding it between the strands of the wire.

15. You can now show off your piece of Baroque jewelry.

"Cluster" Earrings

As the name suggests, the appeal of these earrings lies in creating a "cluster" of wire. With this exercise you will learn the technique of wrapping beads inside a piece. It can also be done without using beads; in this way you can create balls of wire, which are very original when used as beads.

⌐1

You will need copper wire, 0.025" (0.6 mm) in diameter, some colored beads, earring hooks, and a wooden barbeque skewer.

1. Cut a piece of wire 15 3/4" (40 cm) long and wrap it around the stick, without tightening it too much so that it can be removed easily.

⌐2

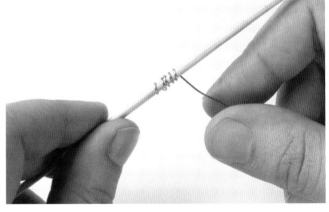

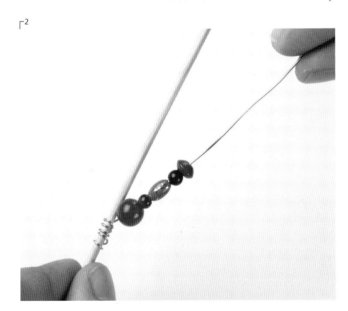

2. String all the beads you are going to use.

3. Begin to twist the stick around itself while letting the beads go slowly.

4. Let all the beads fall around the stick. After, with the leftover wire, continue to wrap up the beads and form a ball.

⌐3

⌐4

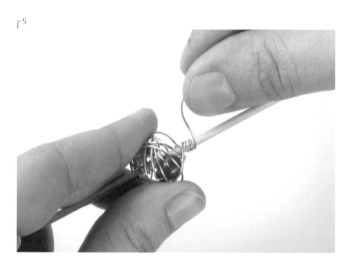

6. Take it off the stick and, with round nose pliers, pull up the last two twists of the spiral.

5. Keep an end at around 3" (7 cm), which will be used to finish off the piece. Twist it around the stick again, making a spiral.

7. Insert the earring hook.

8. The difficulty lies in making two earrings the same. But you can make them almost identical if you are careful to use the same amount of materials for both.

Variations and Examples

From each of the previous exercises you can extract an infinite number of examples and varieties. If you change the size of the wire, the colors or use zinc, silver, brass, aluminum, etc., you can obtain quite varied results, as can be seen in these pieces designed by Elvira López Del Prado.

Also bear in mind the great variety of beads on the market with which you can change the appearance of your jewelry as you wish.

Different grappolo rings in various colors of copper and a wide range of beads.

Variations of rings made with silver wire, turquoise, river pearls, and faceted tupi beads made of Czech glass.

Another way of using this technique is by joining the pieces with chains to create bracelets.

Evening necklace in silver, nickel silver, and Czech glass.

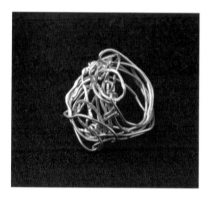

Hammered silver ring made using a jig.

Necklace with spiral pieces and elongated spirals.

"Cluster" bracelet without beads.

"Cluster" party earrings.

"Cluster" earrings.

Earrings made with a jig and different beads.

Costume Jewelry
Made with Felt

Through this
chapter dedicated to felt,
you will see various exercises
done with different techniques.
As wool can be worked dry or wet, in
sheets (industrial felt) or in skeins, exercises
are included in the section on techniques
to help you to better understand the
possibilities that working with this
material offers.

Techniques

The strands in wool have the characteristic of contracting by natural means (water, soap, and friction) until they form a compact and inseparable entity. This process is called felting.

Felt is not only made with wet techniques. There is also the dry felting process, done by using felting needles. Depending on the piece to be made, one or the other of these techniques will be used. You can also work with sheets of felt manufactured industrially. Both types can be found in specialty stores.

Working with Sheets of Felt

Working with sheets of industrial felt is a quicker route, as you skip the arduous task of felting. The stiffness and the consistency of felt depend on its thickness. Therefore, you must keep the thickness in mind when working on your pieces.

Thin felt is ideal for making shapes and figures that need a lot of folds, such as origami work, and for pieces that are not in a place which gets a lot of wear, such as brooches. On the other hand, thick felt is useful for making bracelets, rings and necklaces, as due to its resistant nature it will not shows sign of wear through being rubbed by other clothes.

Joins

The final result of a piece made with felt depends greatly on how the joins are finished—that is, how the pieces are fixed to each other. In most cases you will use super glue, always with care and using something like tweezers to avoid touching the glue with your fingers.

The dyes used for dyeing felt can cause a chemical reaction with super glue, including increasing the temperature at the point of contact of the felt with the glue, even discoloring it. This often happens with shades of purple. It is better to replace the glue with transparent nylon 0.045" (1.15 mm) sewing thread and make stitches of a few millimeters that will be well hidden.

Some examples of what can be achieved with manufactured felt.

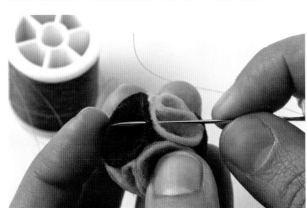

Making it malleable

When you want to make a three-dimensional piece of costume jewelry, with industrial felt, you will need to depend on the main material of the previous chapter, wire.

The procedure is explained with instructions for making a necklace of felt links.

1. As always, match the tools to the materials. In this case, use sheets of thick felt, a medium sized wire, 0.0159" (0.4 mm), and a needle with a large eye, suitable for the thickness of the wire.

2. Cut different strips of felt, some longer than others. And according to the length that you want the necklace to be, cut more or fewer strips.

3. Thread the needle with the wire and pass it through the inside of each of the strips.

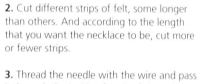

4. Next, cut the ends of all the wires.

5. Carefully, hook the links through each other and stick the ends together with super glue.

6. Once all the links are in place, check that the wire inside is not only providing consistency and durability but also allows you to play with the shapes, as it is now malleable.

7. You have a necklace of links whose shape you can alter whenever you wish.

Felting with Soap and Water

In the wet felting process, the massage you give the material with your hands plays just as important a role as the water and soap you use.

It is advisable to use pine oil soap, as it transforms the water into alkaline and this favors felting. If not, then neutral soap can also be used.

Use very hot water during the process and cold in the final rinse, as these abrupt changes in temperature help the fibers to join.

In the final wash you can add some drops of vinegar to fix the colors.

Beads

Beads are pieces that are very often used in costume jewelry. They are very eye-catching when made in felt and are light, despite their soft compact appearance.

1. A skein of wool, a bowl, a tray, an absorbent towel, a bar of soap, and hot water.

2. Cut some small, equal-sized squares of wool, two layers of which will form a bobble.

3. Put these two layers one on top of the other to give volume and body to the piece.

4. Make it round with your hands to make the work easier. Make all the bobbles you will need now so that you do touch the wool with wet hands later.

5. Wet and soap your hands.

6. Take the bobble and dampen it a little in the hot water.

7. Rotate it in your soapy hands, massaging it lightly. Submerge the bobble in the hot water several times during the process.

8. If cracks appear, add pieces of wool, incorporating them in the same direction as the crack.

9. Continue massaging with soap and water, increasing the pressure with your hands.

10. The last part of the massage consists of pressing down as hard as possible while turning the bobble round.

11. To finish, completely submerge the wool bobble in cold water.

12. A bobble is well made if it is very compact and does not show any cracks when you press it with your fingers.

Drying and piercing

In the summer, the bobbles dry from one day to the next. In the winter, you can use a hair dryer to accelerate the process, put the bobbles on a towel on the radiator—always being careful, or instead put them on a paper towel and wait patiently.

Bobble drying on a paper towel. Before using the bobbles to make a piece of costume jewelry you must wait until they are completely dry, otherwise they will become misshapen.

With a special large-eyed needle, thread the cord and hammer it directly into the bobble. Use flat nose pliers to help you take the needle out. Make the hole right at the moment of making the necklace, as the felt tends to swell up and the hole will not stay open for long.

Strips

Making a felt strip is as simple as constructing a cord of the thickness and length you want. You can use it as a necklace or as an independent piece. You can also use it to make handles for bags made of felt or for hair accessories.

1. To make strips you need a bamboo place mat, like those used to made sushi, skeins of colored wool, an absorbent towel, hot soap, and water.

2. Place the bamboo mat on the towel and prepare a roll of wool with a thickness about two fingers wide and as long as you want to make the necklace. Dampen it well with soap and water.

3

4

3. Next, roll the strip in the bamboo mat and roll it backwards and forwards several times pressing down hard. Repeat this process until you have a strip that is even in size and hardness.

4. Add pieces of wool around the strip, until it has a good amount of volume, and then sprinkle again with soap and water.

5

5. Roll the strip a number of times, until you have achieved a very compact and well stuck together piece.

6. Add a few strands of white wool to decorate it and stick them with soap and water.

6

7

7. After fixing the corresponding clasp, you have a simple necklace made of strips, to which you can add a couple of bobbles made in the same colors.

Felting with Needles

To do dry felting you need to use some special "felting" needles. You can use one needle or a number of them together, depending on the size of the wool. The needles have serrated edges; the fibers tangle around themselves and make the felt.

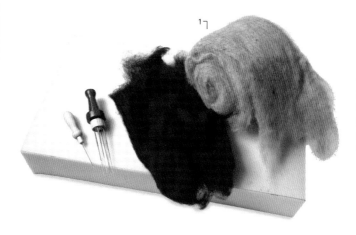

1. All the things that are needed for your work are: a piece of foam for felting, a needle, and a skein of colored wool.

2. Put some layers of wool on the foam, and with the needle hammer them repeatedly, at the same time modeling the shape of a petal. The petal is finished when it acquires a hard consistency. Make three petals of each color like this.

3. When you have them all, fix them to each other by pricking them with the needle. First, those of one color and then those of the other color.

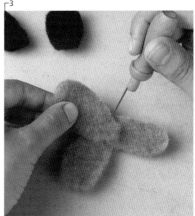

4. Turn them over to fix them properly on the other side.

5. Take a small amount of wool and make a round shape with your hands. Afterwards, place them in the center of the flower, and with the needle prick them until the ball shape is achieved.

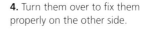

6. When the flower is finished, stick it on the back of a brooch base with super glue.

Filigree embroidery

With the felting needles you can also make detailed and very precise decorations, which are very difficult to achieve with the "wet" technique.

This filigree work is easier to see if it is done at the end on pieces felted with soap and water, as the needles hammer into the wool to fix it to the surface, and if it is not well compacted, the decoration will be buried.

Here, you will see how to decorate some felt bobbles made with water and soap with needles, for which you will need a felting needle and skein and wool.

1. Place a very fine strand of wool on top of the ball and with the needle hammer it softly at first and then more strongly.

2. Work with small strands pressing down on the surface at the same time. Progress will be slow, but the resulting work will be very clean.

3. Now decorate it with spots, choosing small balls and repeat all the previous processes until the pattern is complete.

4. The result is colorful and interesting, and thanks to the felting needles you can achieve almost any decoration that comes to mind, however detailed it may be.

Projects

Throughout this section you will make some pieces based on the different procedures that you have seen with felt techniques, as well as other variations of them.

Firstly, you will make some felt beads coloring the inside so that, when they are cut through, they give you a colored design of circular lines as a result. Next, you will again use the technique of making the sheets of felt malleable, and lastly, you will make a ring out of spirals.

Bead Necklace

With this necklace you can learn various ways of working the wool in one piece, as you make large beads decorated with interior circles, as well as those used for felting.

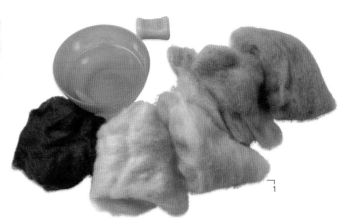

1. For this necklace you will combine orange, bluish-green, turquoise, pistachio, and electric blue colored wool. Use neutral soap and a bowl of very hot water.

2. Following the procedure for making beads with soap and water explained in the techniques section, make six medium beads in pistachio color wool. Next, make another six beads, this time in orange wool and smaller. Also use soap and water.

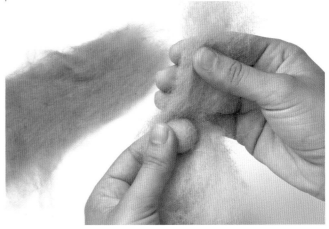

3. Model three more medium-sized beads, in turquoise. Once made, wrap each one in a layer of pistachio wool, which you round with your hands, using soap and water until you have compact beads.

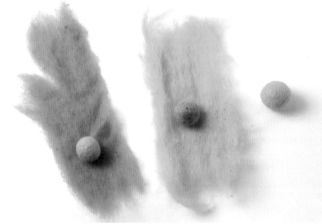

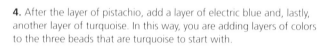

4. After the layer of pistachio, add a layer of electric blue and, lastly, another layer of turquoise. In this way, you are adding layers of colors to the three beads that are turquoise to start with.

5. Once the three beads are ready, cut them through, like disks, into shapes 1" (2 cm) thick, using a knife with a sharp blade.

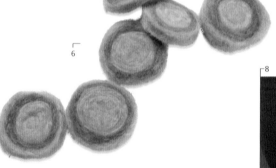

6. You usually get four disks of felt per bead, of which, for this project, you will use the two central ones. So, from the three felt beads you will get six sliced disks.

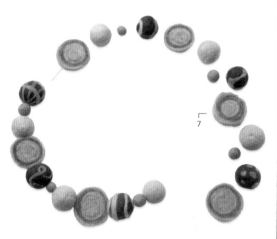

7. Put the pieces in order and pierce them with the help of a sewing needle. In this case, the nylon is 0.0126" (0.3 mm) thick, so you will not need pliers to take the needle out of the beads.

8. A very colorful necklace to brighten up winter afternoons.

Flower Brooch

In this work you will employ a more complicated technique, making sheets of malleable felt. This exercise involves a slightly more elaborate technique, as here you will see how to make an organic shape out of a piece of felt in the form of a flower. You will work with felt sheets of different thicknesses. Lastly, you will learn how to fix the base of the brooch in a professional manner. For this brooch you will will see how to use a paper pattern.

1. Prepare a thin sheet of blue felt, two sheets of thick felt in red and green, super glue, a pin, a needle, 0.0159" (0.4 mm) wire, and the cut out pattern of a flower.

2. Using a pin, fix the pattern of the flower, which you have previously drawn and cut out, to the blue felt and cut it out.

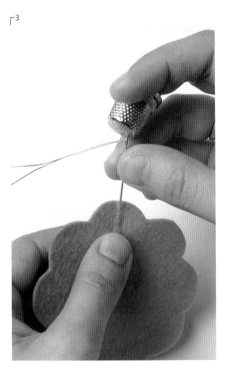

3. Thread the wire through the needle and hammer it through the felt, making it penetrate inside the fibers.

4. Push it into the middle of the flower, take it out, and hammer it back through the same hole.

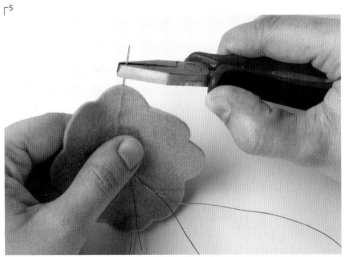

5. Finish the path with the needle until it comes out of the far end from where you started.

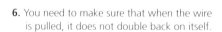
6

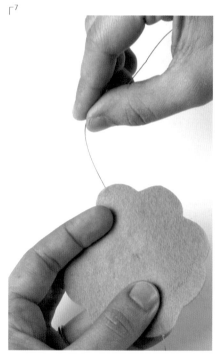
7

6. You need to make sure that when the wire is pulled, it does not double back on itself.

7. Pull the wire to tighten it inside the flower.

8. Cut the leftover ends at the level of the flower, so that the wire stays hidden inside. Repeat this process along the length of the flower at various points.

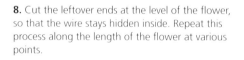
8

9

9. Cut an oval piece of the same size as the base that you are going to put on the brooch, and mark with a pencil where the ends of the brooch will go.

10

10. Make two small cuts with the scissors on the pencil marks and "sink" the brooch into them.

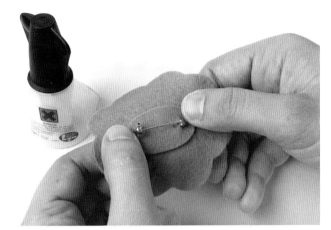

11. Stick it to the flower with super glue.

12. Cut equal-sized strips of green felt, 1/2″ (half a centimeter) thick and 3″ (eight centimeters) long.

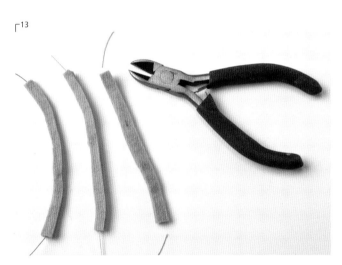

13. Pass wire through the middle of each strip with the help of a sewing needle. Then, cut the leftover ends close to the end of the strips.

14. Cut the strips through the middle with some scissors.

15. Draw a flower in pencil on the red felt and cut it out.

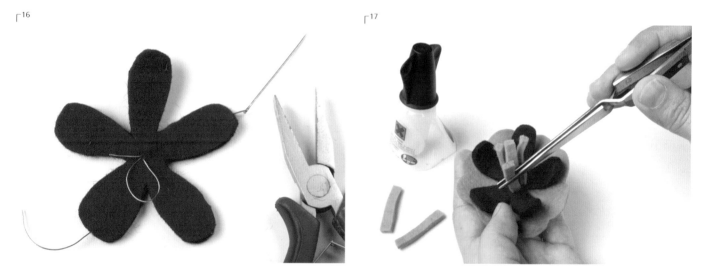

16. Repeat the process of sewing it with wire inside, making it pass through all the petals.

17. Stick both flowers, just in the center, one on top of the other. Lastly, add the pistils in green, sticking them to the base.

18. With your hands, model the flower to give it the shape you want.

Spiral Rings

When beginning with felt, the most basic shapes, like the spiral, are often the first with which to experiment. The spiral is a simple shape but is also elegant and can add a carefree touch to your costume jewelry.

1. Have ready on your table, super glue, some thin sheets of felt in two colors, and a ring base to stick it on.

2. Cut two strips 1/2" (1 cm) thick and 3" (8 cm) long in each color, and cut two more half the length with the same width.

3. Place a long strip in a deep-red color on top of a gray strip.

4. Begin to roll up the end, which only has deep-red felt, until it is totally rolled up.

5. With a drop of glue, join the strips of felt to each other.

6. Repeat the procedure with the color strips the other way round, making another spiral. Again, stick them with glue.

7. Cut a base in a figure eight (the same as the base of the stuck down spirals) and another in a round shape.

8. With glue, join the spirals at the base of the figure eight and, then, join the base of the ring. Cut the circular shape in the middle, sticking each of the parts to the ring. By doing this, you will hide the metal base with felt, giving it a perfect finish.

9. Add some small felt cut offs to decorate the spirals.

Variations and Examples

You have worked with felt using different techniques, all of them easy to make. This is a material that you can combine with others to give pieces a personal and exclusive touch.

The next section shows some pieces of costume jewelry in felt, designed and made by Elvira López Del Prado, which will, without doubt, serve as inspiration to create many others.

Necklace of strips with glass beads. Malleable felt.

Choker of double spirals and flat remnants.

Owl ring with black and white spirals.

Flower ring. Felting with needles.

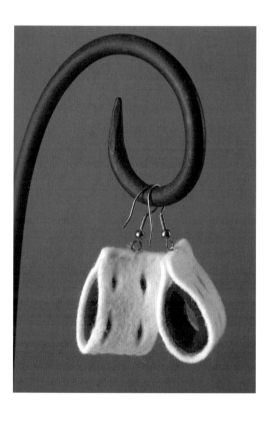

"Cards" earrings. Flat felt.

Necklace of spirals in flat
black and white.

Stripe ring. Sheet felt of different
thicknesses.

Fossil ring (right) and
candy ring (left). Sheet
felt and felted wool.

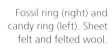

Bracelet of medium beads and pieces
of plastic. Felted wool.

Earrings and ring of cut beads.
Felted wool.

chapter

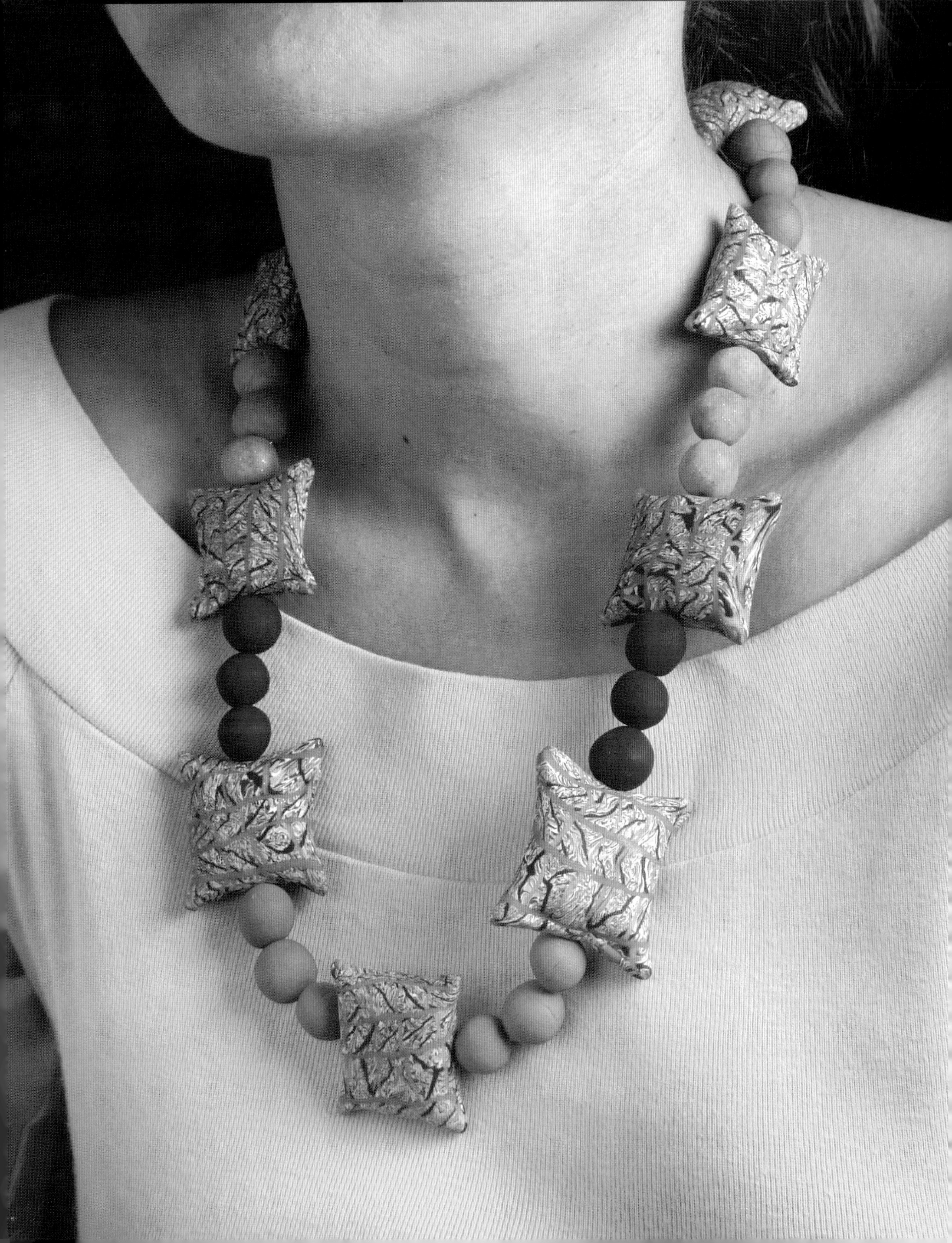

Costume Jewelry
Made of Polymer Clay

Polymer clay is a material used for years by educators for crafts with children. It is easy to find in specialty stores under different brand names. It has an agreeable texture, very similar to traditional Plasticine®. It can be worked with few tools and once the project is finished it only needs to be fired in a domestic oven. If all the manufacturer's instructions are followed, it is not a toxic product.

Techniques

This material lends itself to a multitude of creative uses. The formula was developed in Germany in the 1930s under the name of Fifi Mosaik, and it was designed for making dolls. Later on it came to be called Fimo. Shortly thereafter, it was sold under other brand names. In this chapter, you will find some of the most popular techniques with which craftspeople make their creations, such as the construction of Murano beads, making molds with polymer clay, transferring images, modeling, and, lastly, firing and finishing the pieces made with this material.

The Murano Bead

It is advisable to prepare the clay before working with it. To do this, cut fine slices of clay and pass it through a pasta making machine using the largest setting. A Murano bead consists of joining various strips of polymer clay in different colors in the same piece, balancing them and placing them in such as way that you obtain very diverse designs. Then, you cut very fine slices, with which you cover or wrap beads or any other piece.

The name Murano bead comes from the island of Murano, in Venice. Invented here was the millefiori (a thousand flowers) technique, on which the implementation of Murano beads in the polymer clay is based.

Preparing the clay using a pasta making machine.

Rings and pendants made with Murano beads.

Various examples of Murano beads with different patterns.

Transfers

Before starting any work with polymer clay you need to remember to prepare the clay to be able to work it better. You can transfer images to polymer clay in various ways. Using one method, you can print the desired image onto special cloth transfer paper and stick it to the polymer clay to fire it. If this method is used, it is a good idea to varnish it afterwards.

Another way is to photocopy the image (with a toner photocopier) and give it a thin layer of liquid polymer (sold in a separate container); once fired, remove it patiently. The result is a transparent image for different applications.

You can also apply the photocopied image directly onto the clay without firing, applying water behind and massaging it in, then slowly and carefully

From left to right, three types of transfers: with transfer paper, clay in liquid format, and by direct transfer.

removing all the paper with your fingers. This rubbing will leave just the ink and you will be able to see the image clearly. You can then give it the shape you want and fire it. In this case, you should make a number of photocopies, varying the intensity of the ink, until you achieve the desired image.

If you make the clay into the desired shape, it can be fired at the same time as the paper, so the ink will come off more easily.

Molds

With polymer clay you can also make hard molds (or soft, as you can now buy a special format for molds) for different pieces that, once fired, are easy to reproduce.

To make a mold, the first thing you need is the piece that you want to reproduce. Bear in mind that the mold will be a negative of the piece. For this you can use leftover polymer clay so as not to use new blocks.

To make a mold for a small piece, such as those in the picture, you need a small amount of clay. Make a ball and press it down from the center towards the outside, making sure that you have reached all the corners. Once this is done, take the clay of the piece and fire it (following the manufacturer's instructions).

A good tip for removing the clay without breaking the mold is to put it in the freezer for a few minutes, which facilitates the detachment of the clay, or dust the piece lightly with talcum powder before making the mold.

Detail of a reproduction with a mold.

Set of molds of various pieces.

Modeling

If Murano beads have a great importance in the basics of work in polymer clay, three dimensional modeling constitutes another fundamental part of the process. To model polymer clay, you can use your hands and special modeling sticks as well, which are the same as those used for clay.

You need to prepare the clay beforehand, passing it through the pasta making machine numerous times, and then forming it into the desired shape. Many artists work with polymer clay, modeling it into their creations; for example, they use it to make dolls, household decorations, jewelry, etc.

It is different from clay in that it does not need to be dampened before modeling. Polymer clay is worked just as it is, but you can adopt the techniques used when working with clay to inspire you for your designs.

The next section will explain one of the modeling processes with the creation of some roses, which detail up close a way of understanding modeling, even though there are various modeling techniques.

Modeling roses

Flowers represent a very eye-catching decorative resource, and the texture and colors of polymer clay make the small pieces designed for costume jewelry very realistic. The next section will show how to make a necklace with a triangular composition made of three roses. But with imagination and creativity you can make other patterns by modeling blocks of polymer clay.

1- Prepare three balls the size of a hazelnut in your chosen colors, in this case gold, chocolate brown, and sand. Make two small balls in each color.

2- Flatten them with your fingers.

3- Join them together as shown in the photograph.

4- Continue preparing and flattening the balls of clay, and place them together by overlapping them, giving them shape with your fingers.

5- Continue in this fashion with the other two colors and, carefully, join the flowers together from behind, pressing them down so they stay fixed together well. Then pass a cord through the inside of the piece, which you have previously pierced and fired.

Firing and Finishes

Once the pieces are made, fire them in a domestic oven following the manufacturer's instructions. Generally, they should be put in at a temperature of 266°F (130°C) for fifteen minutes.

It is a good idea to put a piece of aluminum foil on the oven tray, so as not to dirty the clay.

If the pieces are flat, place them directly on the tray, and if they are round you can improvise with a setup like the one in the photograph.

Interior of the oven. With the help of a wire and clothes pegs, put the beads inside the oven. You should always be careful.

Wet sandpapers of different numbers that are used on all pieces. Begin with a low number, 320, for example, and then go up until arriving at a 1000 or 1200, which will take quite a while before achieving a silky feel.

The final step is to apply liquid polish. Use a natural fiber cotton cloth, and give a final massage with a felt cloth to bring the shine out.

Bead made with Murano beads before it is sanded and polished.

Bead made with Murano beads after being sanded and polished

Projects

Through the following three exercises, you will practice the techniques previously explained: modeling, transfers, and Murano beads.

You will begin by making a choker made from chunks of modeled, colored clay. Next, you will make a cameo brooch, where you learn to perform the transfer technique, using special transfer paper, and you will also see one of the uses of the heat gun when applied to polymer clay. Lastly, you will see how to make a Murano bead that imitates cloth, and how to make some beads called pillow beads, because they look just like what they're named after.

Modular Choker

In this step-by-step section you will see how with simple shapes and pure colors you can obtain a fun and summery choker.

1- Make sure you have a knife for cutting clay ready, a punch, four colors of clay, some crimp beads, a bead cap, and a necklace clasp with jump rings.

2- Stretch each of the pieces of colored clay until they are thin and quite long.

3- Give them shape by cutting and modeling them as in the picture.

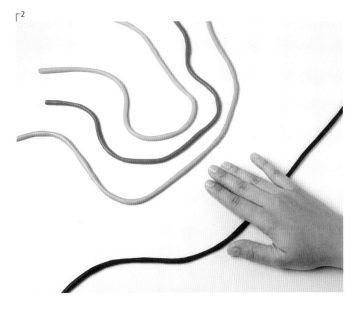

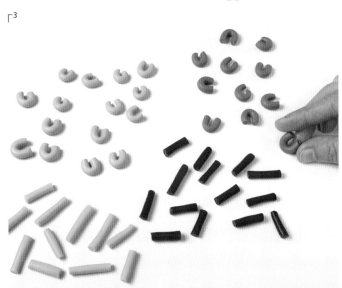

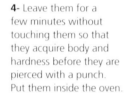

4- Leave them for a few minutes without touching them so that they acquire body and hardness before they are pierced with a punch. Put them inside the oven.

5- Once fired and cooled, pass a 0.02" (0.5 mm) nylon thread through them with the help of a sewing needle.

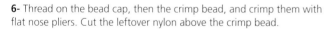

6- Thread on the bead cap, then the crimp bead, and crimp them with flat nose pliers. Cut the leftover nylon above the crimp bead.

7- Close the bead cap with the crimp bead inside to hide it, put the jump ring and the clasp on. Repeat the steps at the opposite end, leaving the necklace very taut.

8- If you vary the shapes, you can personalize it to your taste. In this case, they are imitations of children's sweets.

Cameo Brooch

To make this cameo you are going to use various materials and tools. These are basic requirements and very useful if you are going to begin working with polymer clays. You will need cutters in geometric shapes, clay in liquid format, patinas, and a heat gun.

1- Gather together all the items you need for your work: polymer liquid clay, leftover clay (from other exercises), white clay, asphalt, pasta making machine, heat gun, an oval cutter, a brooch base, and an image printed on transfer paper or cloth.

2- With the machine set at number one, pass the white clay through it and cut two equal sections with the oval cutter.

3- Put the leftover clay, from the cutout oval, between the two white bases. Close it well with your fingers.

4- Using the oval cutter as a guide, cut out the image.

5- Adjust it carefully onto the base with the help of a modeling stick to stop it from getting unsightly wrinkles.

6- Make a thin roll and decorate it with textures using a modeling stick especially designed for this purpose.

7- Fix it to the outside of the cameo.

8- Brush liquid clay all over the surface of the image and spread it with a very soft paint brush or your finger. Fire it for 15 minutes. When you take the cameo out of the oven you will see that it is translucent but not totally transparent.

9- Once fired and cooled, apply hot air with the heat gun; move it backwards and forwards to stop air bubbles forming due to the sudden change in temperature. The result is a transparent and luminous piece.

10- Add it to the brooch base and fire it again.

11- Afterwards, give it a fine coat with asphalt, covering the piece completely, except for the image. Leave it to dry for 24 hours.

12- Johannes Vermeer, master of the Golden Age of Dutch painting, knew how to capture light like no one else. This cameo shows that off, thanks to the chosen image, *Girl with a Pearl Earring*.

Pillow Beads Necklace

A Murano bead imitating printed cloth is the main feature of this necklace. You will also make a type of bead called a pillow bead, due to its characteristic shape.

1- Prepare various blocks of colored clay, a punch, a wooden modeling stick, and a knife for polymer clay.

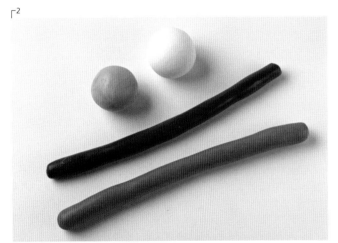

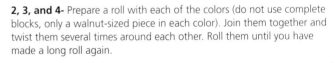

2, 3, and 4- Prepare a roll with each of the colors (do not use complete blocks, only a walnut-sized piece in each color). Join them together and twist them several times around each other. Roll them until you have made a long roll again.

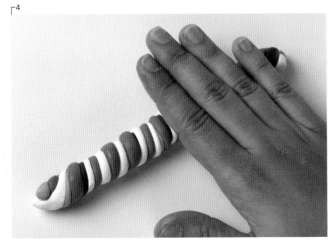

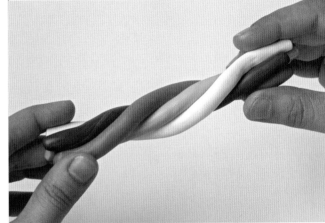

5- Cut them in various pieces of equal length.

6 and 7- Put all the rolls together and repeat the same process a few times until you have achieved a similar effect to the image shown in step seven.

8- Rotate the Murano bead with your hands without pressing down to give it a round shape and make it smaller with the help of a piece of methacrylate, pressing it down on the worktable. You can replace the methacrylate with any object with a flat surface with no texture, such as a CD cover or a small mirror.

9- Once it is reduced, cut it vertically into five parts.

10- Put three colors through a pasta machine on setting number one.

11- Cut rectangles of one of these colors and arrange them as shown in the photograph.

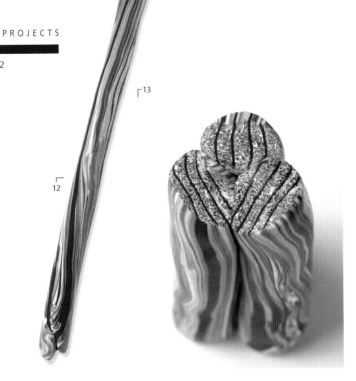

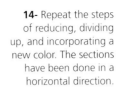

14- Repeat the steps of reducing, dividing up, and incorporating a new color. The sections have been done in a horizontal direction.

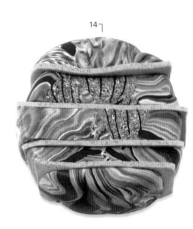

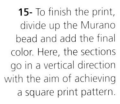

15- To finish the print, divide up the Murano bead and add the final color. Here, the sections go in a vertical direction with the aim of achieving a square print pattern.

12 and 13- Roll the Murano bead again into a roll. Next, divide it into three equal parts, join them together, and roll them together to make it into a rounded shape.

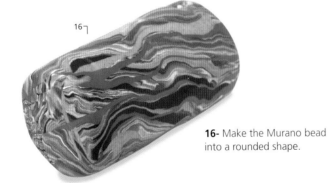

16- Make the Murano bead into a rounded shape.

17- With the help of a of piece of methacrylate make it into a square shape.

18- Cut thin sections, approximately 0.04" (1 mm) thick.

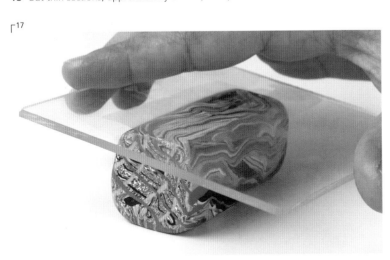

19

20

19- With leftover clay, model a square pillow and put it between the two cut sections.

20- Close the edges.

22

21- Pierce them with a punch.

22- Once fired, sanded, and polished, you will have an attractive and illusory cloth print made entirely of polymer clay.

21

Variations and Examples

Polymer clay is one of the most versatile materials used in costume jewelry. Given its great durability, colorfulness, and plasticity, it allows you to make not only *eye-catching* pieces, but also perfect imitations of other materials, such as finishes, stains, patinas, etc. On these pages you will see some works made in polymer clay created by Elvira López Del Prado, using the techniques seen previously.

Earrings. Polymer clay, paper transfer.

Tuareg rings. Polymer clay.

Arm cuff. Polymer clay.

Imitation cloth bracelet.
Polymer clay.

Roses pendant. Polymer clay and silver leaf.

Millefiori necklace.

Fra Angelico medallion. Polymer clay, gold
leaf, liquid clay, and paper.

Costume Jewelry
Made with Paper and Cloth

The most
common use for cloth is making
clothes and household items, but
recently, it has become fashionable to use
techniques such as patchwork and adapt them to
the worlds of costume jewelry and jewelry.
Equally, you can use traditional decorative techniques
with paper such as *découpage* and apply them to
costume jewelry to obtain very eye-catching results.
In addition to this, paper and cloth can be
combined together and with other materials
to give you new creative inspiration.

Techniques

There are various ways of working with paper and cloth in a simple way, which allow us to create very bright and colorful pieces of costume jewelry. Two of these techniques are *fuxico*, which is a type of patchwork, and *découpage*.

Fuxico has its origins in Brazil, although this technique is also known in the United States as jo-jo patchwork. *Découpage* was an important decorative method imported from France and from the Far East, which became very popular in Victorian England.

With these techniques, you will see how to work with cloth by covering beads, and to use a technique derived from *papier-mâché* applied to costume jewelry.

Fuxico

Fuxico is a technique that has formed part of the traditional crafts of northeastern Brazil for over 150 years.

Fuxico means "intrigue" and, in fact, is a type of patchwork that consists of sewing leftover circles of cloth in an adjoining fashion. This technique was created to take advantage of the remnants of cloth left from making clothes. The joined together circles are used to make bags, bedspreads, pillows, clothes, etc. In the following step-by-step instructions, you will see how to use this technique to also make costume jewelry.

The diversity of shades and color of the cloth used is of prime importance in anything made with patchwork.

Pieces of fuxico of different sizes. They are made from a circular remnant of cloth thorough which a thread has been passed like the diagram shown in the picture.

Découpage

Découpage is a decorative technique that can be used on all types of surfaces: furniture, lamp shades, boxes, etc. The word comes from the French word *découper*, which means "to cut."

The off cuts of decorated paper are stuck to a smooth surface (it can be of any material). Afterwards, they are varnished several times to eliminate any parts that may be sticking up. In this way, the stuck on pieces of paper take on a painted appearance.

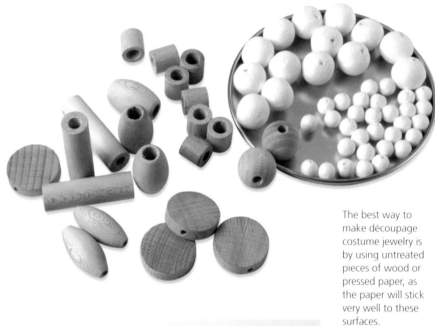

The best way to make découpage costume jewelry is by using untreated pieces of wood or pressed paper, as the paper will stick very well to these surfaces.

It is better to use decorated paper handkerchiefs rather than serviettes or special découpage paper, as it has more cellulose, making it thinner and smoother to work with.

Projects

In the following *exercises* you will do two works in paper and two in cloth. In one of the projects in cloth, you will use the *fuxico* technique to make a necklace, and in the following project you will *see* how to cover balls of pressed paper with cloth to make a fun printed bracelet.

In the paper exercises you will learn to use the delicate technique of *découpage* by making a necklace with wooden pieces and decorated paper handkerchiefs. And lastly, you will create an original bracelet made from tubes of recycled glued paper.

Poppy Necklace

This exercise uses a floral print with a small pattern. So that, when it is cut to go around the wooden beads it will stand out well. This is an important point when seeking out decorated handkerchiefs; the printed pattern should not be too large, otherwise when it is cut and glued the beads, which are usually quite small, cannot be made out clearly.

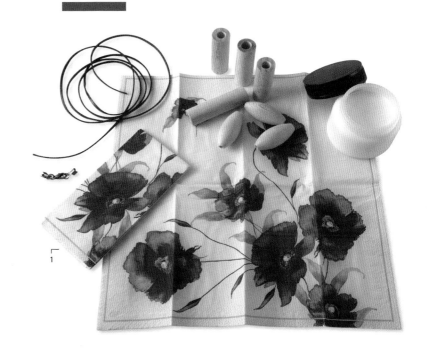

⌐1

⌐2

1- Find some long oval wooden beads, wood glue, a leather cord, a necklace clasp, and a printed handkerchief (here, with a poppy design).

2- Peel off the top layer off the handkerchief carefully so as not to tear it. This layer is the one with the printed pattern on it.

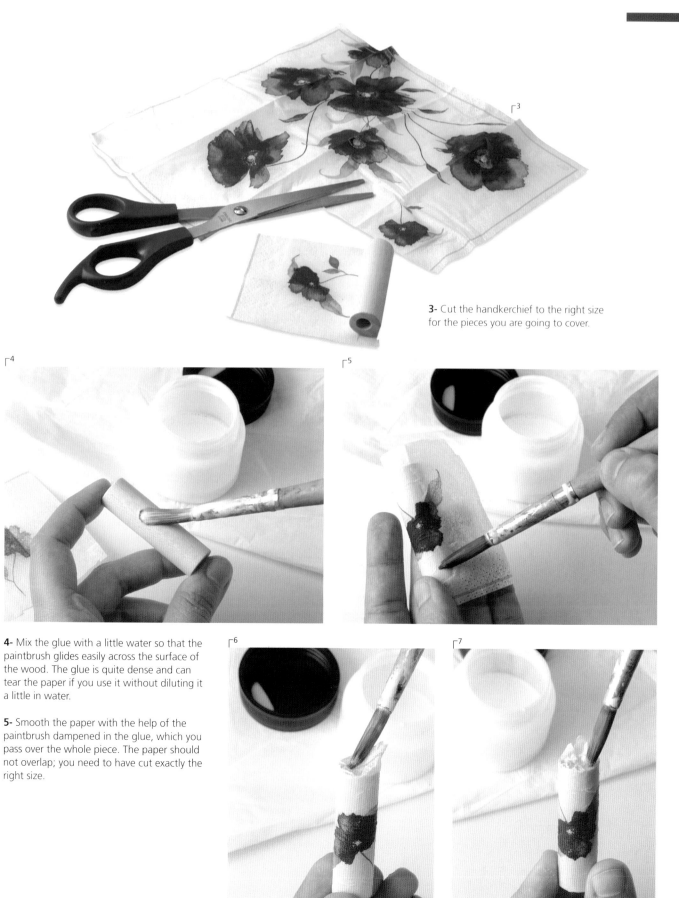

3- Cut the handkerchief to the right size for the pieces you are going to cover.

4- Mix the glue with a little water so that the paintbrush glides easily across the surface of the wood. The glue is quite dense and can tear the paper if you use it without diluting it a little in water.

5- Smooth the paper with the help of the paintbrush dampened in the glue, which you pass over the whole piece. The paper should not overlap; you need to have cut exactly the right size.

6 and 7- We glue the ends of the paper as well, folding the paper with the brush.

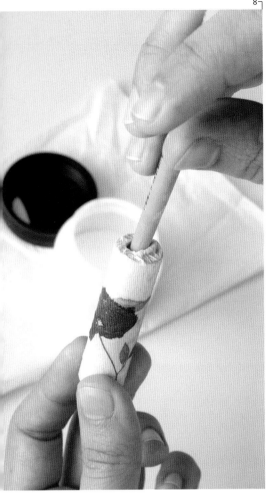

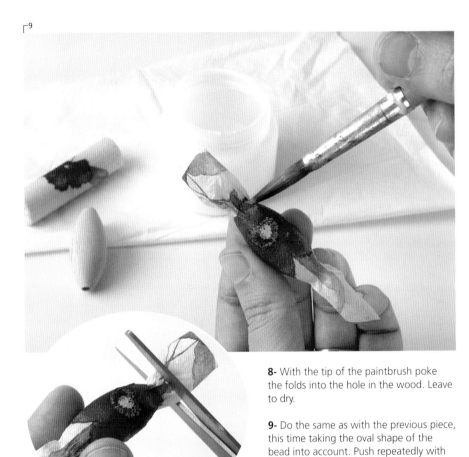

8- With the tip of the paintbrush poke the folds into the hole in the wood. Leave to dry.

9- Do the same as with the previous piece, this time taking the oval shape of the bead into account. Push repeatedly with the paintbrush loaded with glue to soften the paper and avoid unsightly wrinkles.

10- Cut the ends off almost completely.

11- Push what is left of the paper into the holes with the paintbrush well loaded with glue.

12- When the pieces are completely dry, varnish them. The synthetic, transparent, and shiny varnish will give an excellent finish, and protect the pieces from getting damp.

13

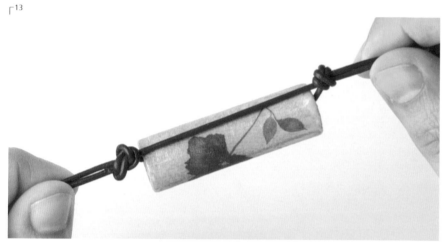

13- Lastly, assemble the necklace together using two leather cords. Pass one through the inside of the wooden bead and the other around the outside. Make a knot between them at the ends of each piece.

14- This is a simple way of putting a necklace together. Here, the beads used have larger holes than others used for costume jewelry.

14

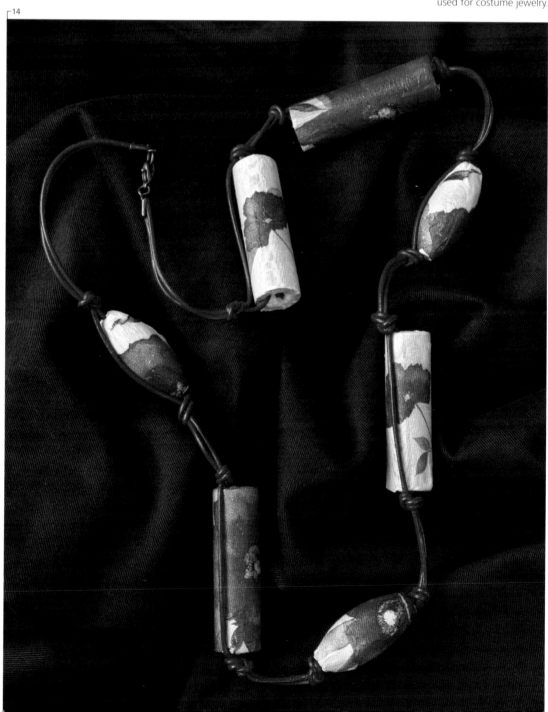

Fuxico Necklace

This design uses a material with a Japanese flower print to make a modern and elegant necklace with the Brazilian *fuxico* technique. Some glass beads have been included in the assembly of the necklace to give it a little weight.

1- Here is an attractive cloth with a Japanese flower print, a leather cord, a reel of thread, some scissors, a necklace clasp, and some glass beads.

2- Cut out the chosen pattern, in this case flowers, into circles.

3- Tack some stitches in a circle 1/2" (1 cm) from the edge of the remnant.

4- Some of the tacking stitches should be longer than others and they should alternate.

5- Tighten the thread to gather up the cloth.

6- Fold the cloth inwards to hide the inside of the piece.

7- Do a double stitch to finish off, leaving the thread hidden.

8- Appearance of some remnants once finished.

9- Join the remnants by stitching them again.

10- Join them together until you have the desired shape.

11- Thread them with a needle threaded with the cord. Pass this inside all the upper pieces and take it out of the other end.

12- Add some glass beads to give weight to the necklace and fix the clasp on. The result is an original Japanese inspired fuxico necklace.

Cloth Bracelet

In addition to working with cloth in different patchwork styles, you can use it to wrap or cover beads. Here, you will see balls of pressed paper and material with a very attractive print.

1- Ready on the work table is the printed cloth, the balls of pressed paper, sewing thread, and elastic thread.

2- Cut a square of cloth for each ball that you are going to cover.

3- Wrap the cloth around the ball.

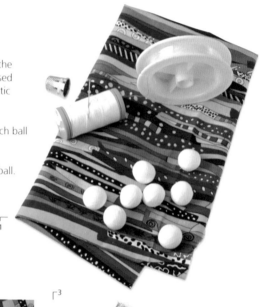

4- Tighten it well, twisting the ball around underneath while securing the cloth above.

5- Make some stitches with the needle and thread to secure the cloth, and finish off with a knot.

6- Cut the ends to even them out.

7- Once all the balls in cloth are finished, pass them onto an elastic thread by using a sewing needle.

8 and 9- An eye-catching bracelet to show off the matching earrings.

Newspaper Bracelet

For this step-by-step exercise you are going to use, almost exclusively, newspaper, which you will afterwards treat with paints and glues to mold it to your taste.

There is a wide selection of cultural, sport, arts, and travel supplements available, just to name a few. From all of these, carefully choose the paper that you wish to use to make this bracelet; try not to use pieces where the letters are legible so as not to decorate your costume jewelry with disagreeable news.

1- Choose some sheets of newsprint and arrange them on the worktable white glue, black acrylic paint, acrylic oils in sepia and black (the acrylic oil can be replaced with normal acrylic paint), a paintbrush, a brush, a nail, and some sticks of wood.

2- The bracelet is made of thick rolls of paper and thin rolls of paper. Begin with the thick rolls, as they take around three days to dry. Make 10 thick rolls around 1" (3 cm) long, for which you will need a strip of newsprint 3 1/2" (9 cm) wide (and the whole length of the newspaper) for each roll. Glue it as shown in the picture.

3- Fold it over into three equal parts.

4- Glue it again and, with the help of a wooden stick dampened in water, roll it up, leaving the stick inside, taking it out when it is totally rolled up. When all the thick rolls are made, remove the sticks and leave the rolls to dry for three days.

5⌐

6⌐

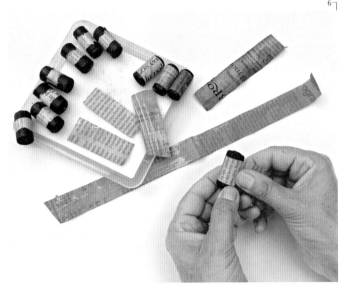

⌐7

5- Once dry, sand them a little with wet sandpaper and paint the edges with black acrylic paint.

6- Wrap the central part of the thick rolls with strips of paper that you have previously colored (in well-diluted acrylic oil) and glued, of about 1" (2.5 cm) wide.

⌐8

7- Now tackle the narrow rolls. For this, paint the newsprint with well diluted acrylic oil. Once dry, cut pieces of about 3 1/2" x 4 3/4" (9 x 12 cm) in your chosen colors (here, sepia and black).

8- Glue and roll up the pieces around a rod as a base (wood or metal) dampened in water, just as you did with the thick rolls, to be able to get them out easily afterwards.

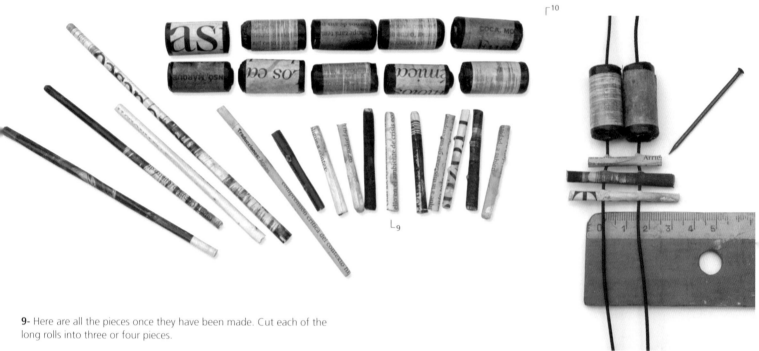

9- Here are all the pieces once they have been made. Cut each of the long rolls into three or four pieces.

10- For the assembly, line up the rolls and pierce them leaving 1/2" (1.5 cm) between each hole; a long nail and ruler will help with this. Once all the rolls have a hole, pass them onto some elastic thread for bracelets, and finish off with two safety knots.

11- When the bracelet is threaded, cut the narrow rolls to adjust the width of the piece. The picture shows two bracelets made with this technique.

Variations and Examples

On this page you will see some pieces that are variations of the techniques explained previously, made by Elvira López del Prado and Ursula Tanner, such as earrings made from printed and glued pieces of paper, necklaces and earrings made from *découpage* combined with other materials such as chains, necklaces made with painted or glued balls of paper, colored paper, and pieces of recycled paper.

Nefertiti necklace. Paper and silver. Piece made by Ursula Tanner, 2007.

Lace earrings. Wood pieces in découpage.

Printed paper earrings.

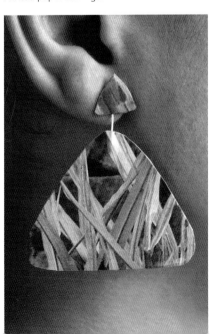

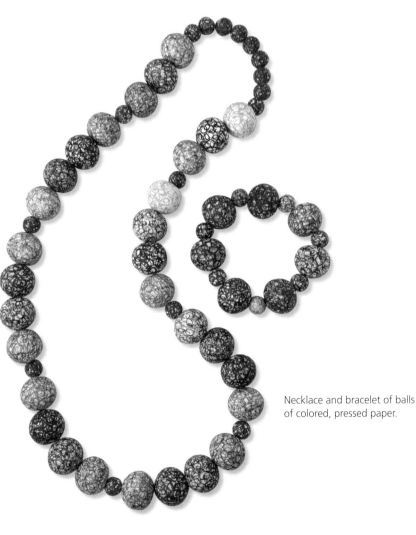

Necklace and bracelet of balls of colored, pressed paper.

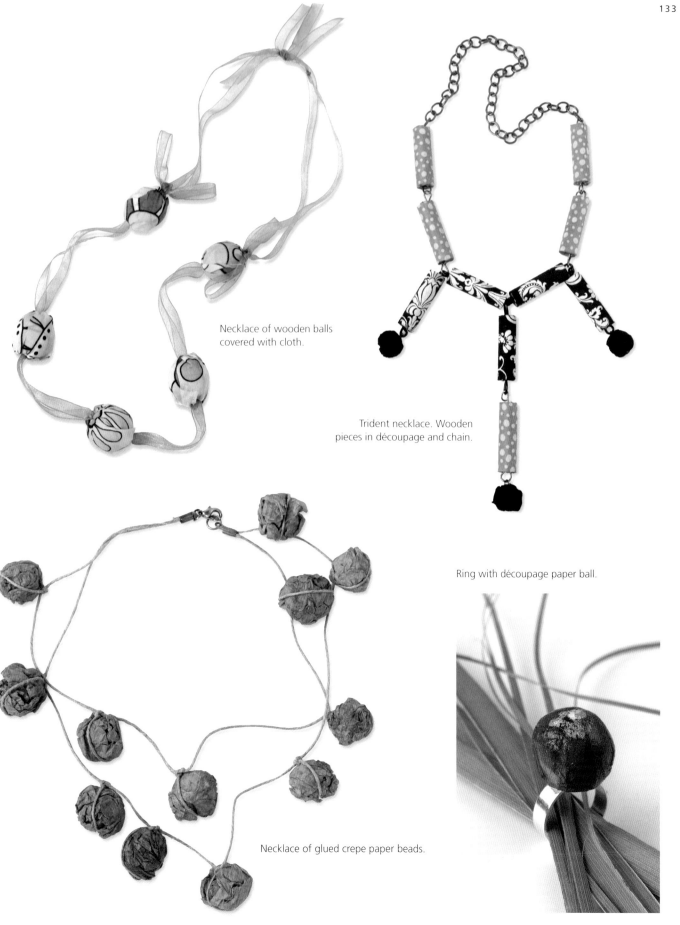

Necklace of wooden balls covered with cloth.

Trident necklace. Wooden pieces in découpage and chain.

Ring with découpage paper ball.

Necklace of glued crepe paper beads.

Artists' Gallery

Throughout these chapters you have learned to work with a variety of diverse materials. Some of them were familiar to you from their everyday household use, such as, paper or cloth. You have seen examples of how to use materials traditionally designed for other uses in costume jewelry, such as wire and felt. And you have delved into new materials like polymer clay.

The following pages will give you a visual tour of work made by artists who work and express themselves through these materials.

Natalia García de Leaniz, Spain. *Bub* Brooch made in polymer clay.

María Joäo Ribeiro, Portugal. Bracelet made in felt.

Angels Cordón, Spain. Ring in wire and glass beads, 2007.

Elitsa Robert, Bulgaria. Set
of various earrings and rings
made in fine wire, 2007.

Kathleen Dustin,
United States.
Victorian Brooch,
brooch made in
polymer clay.

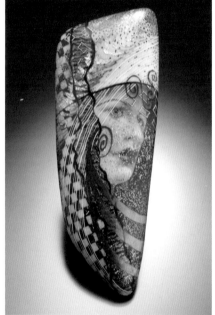

Ana Hagopian, Argentina. *Gauzel Tulip*,
earrings made from paper.

Nel Linssen, Holland.
Bracelets made of paper
on silicon tube, 1997.

María Joäo Ribeiro,
Portugal. Bracelet
made in felt.

Yoko Izawa, England. "E"
Necklace made in cloth.

Cucotoro, Argentina.
Brooches of printed
cloth, 2006.

Elena Relucio, Spain.
Scarf-necklace in felt,
2007.

Cammy Ambrosini, Canada. *Victorian Bouquet*, arm cuff of amethyst,
quartz, tourmaline, smoky and gold thread, 2006.

Anna Osmer Andersen, England.
Chain necklace, old cloth, 2004.

Natalia García de Leániz, Spain. *Watermelon necklace*, made in polymer clay.

Elena Relucio, Spain. Three colored brooch in felt, 2007.

Donna Kato, U.S. Beads made in polymer clay.

Nel Linssen, Holland. Plastic bracelets covered in paper, 1989.

Kathleen Dustin, United States. *Tornado bracelet*, bracelet in polymer clay.

Anette Kortenhaus, Australia. *Zipfel* felt ring—ring made in felt.

Angels Cordón, Spain. Ring in wire with glass beads, 2007.

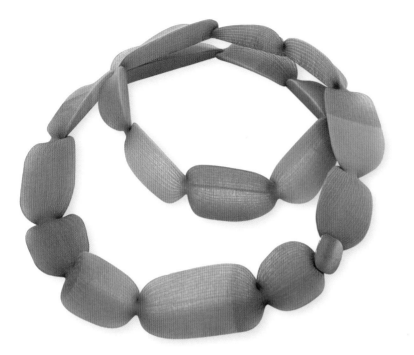

Yoko Izawa, England. *Pebbles* necklace, made in cloth.

Donna Kato, U.S. Inro made in polymer clay.

Noemí Gera, Hungary. *Black Paper Ring*, ring made of paper.

Karen Monny, Paris (France). *Sea Urchins* and *Oyster* brooches—brooches made in silk.

Anette Kortenhaus, Australia. *Tall and fat rings*, rings in papier-mâché and colored paper.

María Sáiz, Spain. Bracelet made in polymer clay and silver.

Glossary

Anvil. Piece of steel-covered iron for hammering metal.

Arm cuff. Bracelet worn a little underneath or above the elbow.

Asphalt. Liquid patina applied to pieces to age or darken them.

Bead. All the small pieces with a hole in them, that are used in making costume jewelry.

Bead caps. Very thin sheet of metal for decorating objects, for example beads.

Coiling rod. Metal tool used to make spirals of metal thread in various sizes.

Costume jewelry. Male and female accessories made with non-precious materials.

Creative process. Path taken by the artist from the initial stimulus that triggers inspiration, leading to the idea for the project, then the design, and finally the piece itself.

Crimp beads. Small metal balls that can be flattened with pliers to hold threads.

Cutters. Pieces of metal in various shapes used to make clean cuts on polymer clay.

Cutting pliers. Useful for cutting metal wire and small metal surfaces.

Découpage. Decorative technique that consists of decorating furniture and objects by careful cutting of decorated paper.

Design. Original concept for an idea expressed in a drawing or model.

Diameter. The measurement of the inside of round pieces, such as copper wire used for costume jewelry.

Draw out. Reduce metal to wire or thread by pulling it into a line.

Earring backs. End or nut added to the back or the hooks of earrings so they do not slide out of the ear.

Ephemeral. Something that lasts for a short time, if the materials used are perishable or because it has not been designed to last.

Felting. Process by which wool is converted into a cloth called felt.

Filigree. Work made by very fine metal threads joined or soldered together to create decorative and visually attractive patterns.

Finding. Set of pieces and accessories that form part of costume jewelry making.

Flat nose pliers. Tool used for holding and crimping.

Heat gun. Tool usually used for stripping that craftspeople use for working with polymer clay.

Inspiration. Stimulus capable of provoking the making of original and creative pieces. Inspiration is something traditionally attributed to artists.

Jig. Tool made of a base with holes and a number of pegs. It is used for filigree work.

Jump ring. Metal wire in a circular shape used to join pieces together and connect them in a chain.

Memory thread. Steel metal thread used to make necklaces, bracelets, and rings, it is in the shape of a spring and is cut to the desired size. The support is usually used with beads.

Merino sheep. A species of sheep found all over the world that has high quality wool.

Methacrylate. A solid transparent plastic material whose smooth surface makes it ideal for working with polymer clay.

Mica powder. Mica is a multiple silicate in various colors found naturally in the ground.

Murano bead. Longish chunk made of different strips of colored polymer clay cut to make decorative patterns.

Neutral soap. Alkaline-free soap that does not contain perfume or colorants.

Nylon thread. A very resistant synthetic thread made in various thicknesses and used in costume jewelry for making necklaces.

Organdy. Cloth with an appearance like muslin used in making pieces of costume jewelry to achieve an elegant finish.

Papier-mâché. A dough created from strips of torn up paper and soaked in water and glue.

Pasta making machine. Kitchen tool used for making fresh pasta. Artists use it to work the polymer clay.

Patchwork. Meaning work made from patches or remnant of cloth, it is a technique used the world over to make all types of items in cloth.

Patterns. Examples that serve as a guide when making another model the same or similar.

Polymer clay. Type of thermoplastic polymer that reacts and stabilizes with a rise in temperature.

Punch. Metal tool finishing in a point for making cuts, indents, and holes.

Ring measurer. Hard tube with marks to mark the size and diameter of rings.

Rod. Basic tool for making costume jewelry. Used to insert beads.

Round nose pliers. Tool for opening and closing jump rings, doing filigree work, and making circles.

Rubbing. Act of rubbing pieces of wool that will then make felt.

Sandpaper. Special paper of a particular weight designed to smooth rough surfaces. The weight is shown on the back with a number; the lower the number, the higher the grain and vice versa.

Sketch. All the drawings and notes made before putting an idea in concrete form.

Still life. Composition, usually in a picture, where there is a collection of objects in the foreground accompanied by other elements.

Super glue. An adhesive suitable for sticking all types of materials thanks to the speed with which it dries.

Synthetic varnish. Solution of various liquid substances that dry and harden when exposed to the air. It is applied to surfaces to protect them from the weather.

Tiger tail. Cable wire made of steel covered in nylon, used to make necklaces when the wire forms part of the design of the piece.

Tools. All the objects needed to make something.

Transfer. The transfer of an image on printed paper to polymer clay.

Wire. Metal thread obtained by drawing out.

ACKNOWLEDGMENTS

The author wishes to thank:
Parramón Press, especially María Fernanda Canal, for her confidence in me to produce this book.
Joan Soto for practical advice on photography and composition.
The independent photographers for each artist, the generous permission to use their images.
Mª Carmen, for her advice and kindness.
Ursula Tanner for her collaboration on the chapter dealing with paper.
ursulapapereciclat@yahoo.es

To the collaborating artists:
Natalia García de Léaniz
Jewelry designer
www.tatanatic.com
Madrid, Spain
Ana Hagopián
Jewelry designer
www.anahagopian.com
Barcelona, Spain
Alyssa Dee Kraus
Jewelry designer
www.alyssadeekrauss.com
U.S.
Anette Kortenhaus
Jewelry designer
www.anettekortenhause.com
Australia
Angels Cordón
Jewelry designer
Angels.cord@gmail.com
Barcelona, Spain
Anna Osmer Andersen
Jewelry designer
Osmer75@yahoo.com
England
Arthur Hash
Collateral Faculty sculpture and extended media crafts painting and printmaking.
Virginia Commonwealth University
www.arthurhash.com
U.S.
Burcu Büyücünal
Jewelry designer
www.burcubuyucunal.com
Turkey
Cammy Ambrosini
Jewelry designer at www.Bejigged.com
Newfoundland, Canada
Cucotoro by Inés Barbón and Sebastián Solveyra
Costume jewelry and accessories designers
www.cucotoro.com
Buenos Aires, Argentina
Elena Relucio Arias
Jewelry designer
www.blogs.ya.com/elenarelucio
Spain
Elitsa Robert Altanova
Jewelry designer
Elitsa.r@gmail.com
Bulgaria
Ineke Otte
Designer and artist
www.inekeotte.nl
Holland
Joan Scott
Textile artist
Joanthomasscott@msn.com
U.S.
Dominic Desmons
Karen Monn Paris, fashion accessories
www.westerndesign.fr/karenmonny
Paris, France
Kathleen Dustin
Jewelry designer
www.kathleendustin.com
U.S.
María Ribeiro
Graphic designer
www.flickr.com/photos/p0250q
www.kjoo.etsy.com
Portugal
Natalie Lleonart
Jewelry designer
www.nit.bigpondhosting.com
Australia
Nel Linssen
Jewelry designer
www.nellinssen.com
Holland
Noemí Gera
Jewelry designer
Noja1002@freemail.hu Hungary
Sarah Kate Burgess
Jewelry designer
www.adorneveryday.com
U.S.
Yoko Izawa
Jewelry designer
y_izawa@yahoo.co.uk
England
María Saiz
Artist and jewelry designer
http://www.flickr.com/photos/7201667@N03/
Spain

Thanks go to the Barbara Berger Foundation, Mexico, for the use of images of its pieces of costume jewelry for this book.

Elvira López Del Prado Rivas
Jewelry designer and teacher of costume jewelry
www.lopezdelprado.com
www.cursosdebisuteria.com
Barcelona, Spain

I want to dedicate this book to Jeremy, my husband, and to my daughter Claudia, and to thank my mother and my sister for their invaluable help.